JOHN HENRY
NEWMAN
Prayers · Poems
Meditations

JOHN HENRY
NEWMAN
Prayers · Poems
Meditations

Selected and Introduced by

A · N · WILSON

CROSSROAD • NEW YORK

1990

The Crossroad Publishing Company
370 Lexington Avenue
New York, NY 10017

Introduction and compilation copyright © 1989 by A. N. Wilson

Printed in Great Britain

Library of Congress Cataloging-in-Publication Data

Newman, John Henry, 1801-1890.
  [Selections. 1990]
  Prayers, poems, meditations/John Henry Newman; selected and
introduced by A.N. Wilson.
     p. cm.
  ISBN 0-8245-1004-6
  1. Devotional calendars—Church of England.   2. Devotional
calendars—Catholic Church.   3. Church of England.   4. Anglican
Communion.   5. Catholic Church.   I. Wilson, A.N., 1950-   .
II. Title.
BV4811.N525   1990
242'.2—dc20   89-29913
                                                       CIP

Contents

For S. P. B.

Introduction

John Henry Newman was born in London in 1801. He died in Birmingham in 1890. His long life divides neatly into two parts: the first forty-five years were spent in the Church of England, and the second forty-five years in the Church of Rome. Only in our own generation has it been recognized how much Newman helped to change both Churches by his writings and preachings.

His family were believers in what he later called Bible Christianity; neither especially high church nor especially low. His father was a banker whose fortunes declined when the bank collapsed. Mr Newman went to manage a brewery in Hampshire; and when that failed, he appears to have become a publican in Clerkenwell. But in spite of financial worries, Newman's family life appears to have been a constant source of happiness to him. He was the eldest boy, and he tells us that he was a poetic child who used to wish that the Arabian Nights Tales were true; 'I thought life might be a dream or I an angel, and all this world a deception, my fellow-angels by a playful device concealing themselves from me, and deceiving me with a semblance of a material world.'

When he was fifteen, Newman underwent a profound conversion experience, and thereafter he followed a rigidly Calvinistic and dogmatic view of Christianity. Even as an old man, he would say that he had never entirely lost the Calvinistic view that the elect were a very small band, nor the superstition that the 144,000 who people heaven in St John's Apocalypse represent the actual number of people alive on this earth at any one time who were saved.

This imaginative boy, who liked nothing better than to lose himself in music (he was an accomplished violinist and in later life composed a violin sonata) was also, from the beginning, someone who thought of himself as a writer. As a schoolboy he wrote essays, modelling his style on that of Addison, and he composed verses throughout his life. A very typical piece of Newman's prose was written when he was only eighteen:

Bells pealing. The pleasure of hearing them. It leads the mind to a longing after something I know not what. It does not bring past years to remembrance. It does not bring anything. What does it do?

We have a kind of longing after something dear to us and well known to us, very soothing.

This inner, and highly romantic Newman was not the whole man. He was good at mathematics. He enjoyed the process of reasoning for its own sake, and it was no surprise that, when he finished school, his father should have wanted to send him to a university. (This was before the family lost all their money.) In a haphazard way, they chose to send the boy to Oxford. It is said that even as the post-chaise waited at the door they had not decided whether to send him to Oxford or Cambridge, until a curate at St James's Piccadilly recommended them to try Oxford. Newman was accordingly sent to Trinity.

As an intensely shy, homeloving, priggish boy of sixteen, he found the rowdyism of his fellow-collegians very hard to stomach. Also, he overworked, worried about his examinations in a fruitless way, and failed to get a decent degree. In spite of this, he was brave enough to try the fellowship exam at Oriel College. His brilliance was recognized and he was made a fellow on 12 April 1822. Newman felt it to be 'the turning point of my life and of all days most memorable'.

It was memorable, because Oriel was the most distinguished college, intellectually, in the entire university, and because the subjects taken seriously there were precisely those which appealed to Newman's mind: that is to say, they were religious subjects. Some of the fellows were theological 'liberals' who believed that Christianity, if it was to survive in the nineteenth century, must adapt itself to the changing conditions of modern times and modern intellectual discovery. Other fellows, in a minority at first, but growing in number during Newman's time there, took the opposite view. Young Edward Bouverie Pusey, for instance, who was elected to an Oriel fellowship not long after Newman, was one of the few Oxford men who had read the modern German critics of the Bible. They were trying to read the Bible in a dispassionate way, as if it were any ancient text. Pusey, initially tempted by this approach, felt that it would end in complete unbelief, and he threw himself entirely behind those Oriel fellows who believed that religion was essentially a revealed thing, given to us by God, and that it is our duty as Christians to accept what we are told by the Church and to respond to God's revelation with lives of inner holiness. The leading exponent of this latter point of view was John Keble, famed today as the poet of *The Christian Year*, from which many popular hymns ('Blest are the pure in heart', 'New every morning is the love') are drawn. In his day, Keble was seen as some kind of saint, and his opinions about the state of the Church and the nation were taken extremely seriously.

Newman responded emotionally to the influence of Keble, and he soon discarded his old Calvinist low-church standpoint. But he probably absorbed more than he quite realized of the 'liberal' standpoint of such fellows as Thomas Arnold, the famous headmaster of Rugby. At Oriel, he was to spend over twenty years thinking the Christian religion through. Inevitably, many of the things which those Oxford dons considered important now strike us as matters of the utmost triviality. When Parliament proposed to reduce the number of (Anglican) Irish bishops, the high-church fellows of Oriel reacted in a way which might have seemed exaggerated if the Lord Chancellor had proposed the abolition of the Apostles' Creed. But they did so because a principle was at stake: the principle of the Church itself. Was the Church of England merely a department of a secular State which could change the structure and discipline of the bishoprics at will? Or was the Church a direct continuation of that divine society founded by Jesus Christ, with the twelve Apostles as the pillars and Christ himself as the cornerstone?

Modern readers will decide for themselves whether this question, which was so overwhelmingly important to Newman, is an answerable one. It was the personal example of Keble which first brought the question to life in Newman's mind. Corrupt and stodgy as the Church of England might have appeared in many of its manifestations, Keble found in its formularies, its worship, its Prayer Book, a home in which it was possible to practise the Catholic faith as it is found in the Latin and Greek Fathers of the early Christian centuries. The love of Keble was one of the strongest forces in Newman's life. 'His happy magic made the Anglican Church seem what Catholicism was and is,' Newman wrote.

The established system found to its surprise that it had all its life been talking, not prose but poetry. Beneficed clergymen used to go to rest as usual on Christmas Eve and leave to ringers, or sometimes to carollers, the observance which was paid, not without creature comforts, to the sacred night; but now they suddenly found themselves, to their great surprise, to be 'wakeful shepherds'; and 'still as the day came round' 'in music and in light' 'the new-born Saviour dawned upon their prayer' . . . The parish church had been shut up, except for vestry meetings and occasional services, all the days of the year but Sundays . . . but churchgoers were now assured that 'Martyrs and Saints' 'dawned on their way'; that the absolution in the Book of Common Prayer was 'the Golden Key each morn and eve' and informed moreover at a time when the Real Presence was all but forgotten or denied of 'the dear feast of Jesus dying, upon that Altar ever lying, while Angels prostrate fall' . . . Such doctrines coming from one who had such claims on his readers from the weight of his name, the depth of his devotional and ethical tone, and the special gift of consolation, of which his poems themselves were the evidence, wrought a great work in the Establishment.

It was as the disciple and follower of Keble that Newman undertook his great work in the Church of England as Vicar of the University Church in Oxford, St Mary's, and preached that marvellous series of sermons from which much of this book is drawn. Newman always read his homilies, and, distrustful now of his emotional evangelical past, he contrived to put as little histrionics into the performance as possible. But this very fact, that the profound religious emotion of Newman's heart was held rhetorically in check, made the sermons all the more powerful. Undergraduates and dons poured into St Mary's each Sunday afternoon to hear him expound the Scriptures and to spell out the searching demands of Christ. He probably never wrote prose more polished or careful than these sermons, and they have claims to be the most superb pieces of religious prose in the English language. Matthew Arnold, destined to be Keble's successor as the Professor of Poetry at Oxford, has left a famous memory of those sermons. 'Who can forget the charm of that spiritual apparition, gliding through the dim afternoon light of St Mary's,' he asked, 'rising into the pulpit, and then breaking the silence with a spiritual music, subtle, sweet, mournful?'

Keble and Newman made the Catholic religion seem like a romance, and the generation who were up at Oxford during the 1830s were carried away with it, in rather the way that leftwing politics obsessed the undergraduates of the 1930s. Just as, in the 1930s, older people feared that the young were being seduced by doctrines which were in reality Soviet Communism in disguise, so, for the grown-ups of the 1830s, there was the fear that Newman's Anglo - Catholicism was really Roman Catholicism in disguise. He and his friends produced a series of pamphlets, known as *Tracts for the Times*, expounding the Catholic teaching which they believed to be the Church of England's true birthright.

Throughout this period, Newman was reading deeply in the Fathers of the Church – Clement and Origen of Alexandria, St Augustine, Gregory of Nyssa, and others. He did not realize at first that he was playing with fire. The more he read, however, the less Keble's dream rang true, the less able Newman was to see the primitive Catholic Church in the modern Church of England. He tried to do so, and his most extreme attempt was in the Ninetieth of the *Tracts for the Times*, in which he argued that there was nothing in the Thirty-Nine Articles (the apparently Protestant definition of faith in the Prayer Book to which all undergraduates, as well as all beneficed clergymen had to subscribe) which was incompatible with Catholicism. Even such belligerently Protestant articles as Number XII condemning 'the Romish Doctrine concerning purgatory' were, Newman said, only condemning modern Roman Catholic abuses. The doctrine of Purgatory itself was perfectly admissible for Anglicans.

Newman's Tract Ninety caused a storm of protest, and all the heads of houses save one united to condemn it. Thereafter, Newman's Oxford career was in ruins. He withdrew from university life and preached no more at St Mary's. In an outlying village of Oxford, Littlemore, which was attached to the parish, Newman spent nearly three years with a group of friends, living a life of austere religious simplicity, writing his book on *The Development of Christian Doctrine*, and contemplating what to do next.

The Development of Doctrine is a very distinctively Newmanian idea. On the one hand it is profoundly authoritarian and traditional; for it is a justification of the Church rather than the Scriptures as the great arbiter of doctrine. On the other hand, modernists and liberals have been able to find in the idea that doctrine can change and develop a *raison d'être* for a deeply untraditional form of belief; for if it is conceded that the Spirit can reveal to later generations doctrines which at the beginning were only implicit, there is no logical reason why we may not see the Spirit at work in the faculty of human reason. Newman's development idea rescues the modern Christian from fundamentalism and obscurantism; but that is not how or why he evolved it. Once he had seen that Christian belief did in fact differ from age to age, with new ideas unfolding all the time, some of them being accepted as orthodoxies and others rejected, it became of paramount importance to decide whether this process of selection was purely arbitrary or whether there in fact existed on earth a divinely established office vested with the authority to lead the world into all truth. The Scriptures relate that such authority was given to the Apostles by Christ when he told them to go and teach all nations. But had this authority vanished in the apostolic age, or was it existent yet?

No Anglican, however well-disposed towards his bishops, could pretend to find in these lawn-sleeved individuals, sitting in the House of Lords, the apostolic figures whom Newman sought. Nor would they have claimed such apostolic authority for themselves. But the Catholic bishops, and the see of Rome above all, did make such claims; and the more he meditated and prayed about the matter, the more Newman concluded that the Roman Church was indeed the Fold of the Redeemer. On 9 October 1845, he dismayed his many Anglican followers and friends by joining the Roman Catholic Church.

The next forty-five years of life were to be very different. In 1845, the Roman Catholic Church in England was extremely small. It was made up chiefly of the tiny number of old Catholic families who had not changed their religion at the time of the Reformation (these were mainly in the North) and the immigrant population, chiefly from Ireland, who had come to escape the famines. Neither category had much in common with Newman, and it was hard for the Catholic authorities to know what to do with him. Newman's conversion was hugely influential on the Anglican Church. Many followed him, and among those who did, figures like Frederick William Faber, W. G. Ward and Henry Manning, had a very different idea of the Catholic religion from Newman's own. They were what was called 'ultra-montanes', meaning, 'beyond the mountains' – i.e. the Alps. In terms of piety they wished to imitate all the more florid excesses of Italy. In the ideas of church discipline they were almost belligerently support-ive of papal authority, not merely in the spiritual realm, but as a temporal thing. This group of converts together with priests of Irish extraction came to dominate the English Roman Catholic Church in the middle and late years of the century, and they did not find Newman's much more subtle Catholicism, derived largely from reading the early Fathers of the Church, particularly congenial. They suspected him of being wishy-washy, even heretical, and the various tasks he was assigned in the Roman Catholic Church were all in different ways failures.

He established the Oratory at Birmingham on the pattern of St Philip Neri's Chiesa Nuova in Rome. But, Newman was to write, 'I prefer English habits of belief and devotion to foreign . . . In following those of my own people, I show less singularity, and create less disturbance than if I made a flourish with what is novel and exotic.' Faber, on the other hand, was an exotic. Weeping madonnas, tearful Marian hymns, lace and birettas were, for him, the very hallmarks of Catholic devotion; and these were but the outward manifestations of a deep division of temperament between himself and Newman. There was no point in their trying to go on together and eventually the greater part of the Oratorian community left Newman in Birmingham and went to found their own Oratory at Brompton in London, where to this day it keeps alive a splendid tradition of baroque worship and practice.

Newman's religion found architectural expression in the church he built for the newly-founded Catholic University in Dublin, where he became the first rector. The church on St Stephen's Green is modelled on the old basilican churches of Ravenna, and harked back to the time of the Arian controversies about which he had made himself an expert in happier Oxford days. Its Latinity is early, its numinous character is quiet, mysterious, strange rather than being loud or triumphalist. It speaks of Newman's profound sense of God as the Ultimate Mystery before whom we can only kneel in awed silence. It reminds us too, not a little, of the child Newman, who believed this world a dream and himself an angel.

Newman's time in Dublin, where he delivered that magnificent series of lectures on education which were to receive the title *The Idea of a University*, was very unhappy. He missed his Oratorian friends in Birmingham, he was distrusted by the Irish, and he fell out with the Archbishop of Dublin, Dr Cullen. It was a relief to get back to England. But among English Catholics, he encountered the same spirit of misunderstanding and mistrust. He was editor of a periodical called *The Rambler*, but found himself so violently attacked in its rival, *The Tablet*, that for the sake of quiet, he resigned. Rumours flew about that Newman was disillusioned with Catholicism and that he was planning to return to the Church of England. He never truly felt tempted to do so because he was always quite clear in his mind, from the time of his conversion until his death, that Roman Catholicism was true. But it was a hard ride.

When Newman was sixty-three, another attack came his way, this time from that muscular Christian and author of *The Water Babies*, Charles Kingsley. Writing a review in *Macmillan's Magazine*, Kingsley suggested that Newman had been a liar during his Anglican ministry, that 'truth for its own sake was never a virtue among the Roman clergy', and that Newman had in fact been a crypto-papist all along. Now, the great principle of Newman's life was the love of truth, and the most distinctive feature of his intellectual view both of human life and of history was that of change. He was fascinated by how people change, and how societies change. He himself had changed most extraordinarily, and Kingsley's crude suggestion – that if Newman was now a Catholic he must always secretly have been a Catholic – called out of Newman his best book, 'A Defence of His own Life', the *Apologia pro Vita Sua*.

He had never written like this before for the public. The poise, and much of the irony of his public manner, which so baffled and enraged his critics, was laid aside. He wrote the story of what had been going on inside his head since he was a small child. He wrote the whole story of his love affair with Oxford, his continuing devotion to those High Church friends who had not been able to join him on the road to Rome, his gratitude to the friends who had done so and, above all, his unshaken belief in the religion which he had adopted. He was kind enough not to let the public know what a difficult time he had been given in the Roman Church, above all by his fellow-converts Manning and Ward. But if there was suppression of the truth in this one small area, there was no doubting the burning sincerity and intellectual integrity of the man. And the book is full of a sort of poetry. He wrote it in tears, very rapidly, and the famous passages, such as his memory of the snapdragons growing opposite his freshman's rooms at Trinity, never fail to move. Although the hardline ultramontanes disliked the *Apologia* intensely, because it seemed to make out that religion was not a matter of authority, but something going on inside your head, the book had a tremendous success. Christians of all kinds – Anglicans, Nonconformists and Catholics – recognized it as a genuine pilgrimage, lived quite sincerely in the belief that God, as in Newman's most famous poem, was leading him on 'O'er moor and fen, o'er crag and torrent, till the night is gone.'

Newman, after the *Apologia*, became a slightly different man. Though still disconcertingly ready to take offence, he was now much more reassured of a wide body of public interest and support. Though ever engaged (to a modern eye dismayingly so) with ecclesiastical controversy, he was in a position much more to address himself to the big religious question. In public disputes with Dr Pusey he was to carry on debating the catholicity of the Church of England. With Manning he would damage his chances of promotion in the Roman Church by taking a quizzical view of ultramontane claims, and with the likes of Faber he would continue to uphold a more austere, 'patristic' Catholicism as opposed to the lace and madonna type of religion. But all these areas of concern were trivial compared with the question of whether or not there is indeed a God, whether our moral impulses were of divine origin or whether they were merely utilitarian compromises made up for the convenience of society.

Though for the greater part of Newman's life he had been involved in the esoteric and sometimes unedifying business of church controversy, it was a period in the world at large of revolutionary change in the development of religious thought. Most thinking people until the second half of the nineteenth century were prepared to accept the notion that the material universe, in all its intricacy and apparent design, argued the existence of a creator, or designer. This was one of the great 'evidences' of Christianity put forward by Paley. Charles Darwin's *Origin of Species*, published in 1859, showed that there was no necessity to posit a Creator as the explanation of how the universe came into being.

Archaeologists and geologists had already discovered that the traditional creation myth in Genesis could not possibly be true in the manner that, say, Pusey believed it. Until that generation, Christians did actually believe that God had fashioned the earth, like a child playing with plasticine, during a specific period of six days. Some time later – in the autumn of 4004 BC, according to a widely-accepted dating – there had occurred, in a place called Eden in Mesopotamia, an historical event called the Fall during which Man – who had been made out of the dust of the earth – had fallen from God's favour.

The scientists had shown that this was simply untrue. Man had evolved over many generations from his cousins the apes. The earth had not been suddenly made like a toy. It too had evolved. These discoveries, together with the knowledge that the Bible itself had grown up like any other ancient group of texts over a large number of years had a shattering effect on most thinking people a hundred and more years ago. Among the towering intellects of Victorian England, nearly all succumbed either to actual unbelief or to some form of agnosticism: Thomas Carlyle, Charles Darwin, George Eliot, Herbert Spencer, John Stuart Mill, Matthew Arnold, none were untouched by the new discoveries. And where did this leave God? Where did it leave the religious impulse, which most of us recognize in ourselves? Where did it leave our moral sense? Was it indeed to be true, as a contemporary Russian novelist was asking, that 'if God does not exist then everything is permitted'? Was a new age dawning, not merely of atheism, but of moral anarchy?

Newman was the only 'intellectual' in the same league as these others whom I have mentioned, who retained religious belief. It is hard to know whether he suffered what a modern person would call 'doubt' – as, say, his brother Francis did, who was an atheist. ('Our blessed Saint Francis', George Eliot called him.) John Newman would certainly have regarded it as sinful to flirt with atheistic ideas, but it has been rightly said that 'it would be possible to compile a manual of unbelief from the asides in Newman's writings'. He understood, as few religious people of the nineteenth century did, what the difficulties were for the unbeliever. He also understood what truly formidable questions faced the world if the unbelievers were right. And because his experience had taught him quite a lot about 'the error and bad taste of the multitude' he did not expect the future of society to be very rosy. His remaining days were therefore devoted to a justification of religious belief itself, published under the title of *A Grammar of Assent*, and an attempt to work out, with his friends in the Catholic Church, an informed, quiet, strong religion which could withstand the coming assaults.

A Grammar of Assent says as much as any book can say by way of intellectual justification for Christian belief. Believers are likely to find it disturbing precisely for that reason. Newman is honest enough to recognize that there is nothing which could prove the existence of God, and very little which can indicate his presence to us – very little that is to say, unless we are prepared to be attentive to those inner promptings by which religious insight or experience might be tested. In so far as he attempts an argument by 'probability' he uses arguments not from the Catholic scholastic philosophers but from the eighteenth-century Anglican Bishop Butler, and from those 'noetic' philosophers who were in vogue when he first went to Oriel. In so far as he argues on a deeper level, he draws less from the *magisterium* of the contemporary Church than from the wells of his own lifelong religious experience and commitment. *A Grammar of Assent,* when stripped of its obvious contemporary preoccupations, is a strangely modern book, perhaps more modern than Newman himself realized.

It shows us very clearly that religious questions are not really answerable, or even meaningful, outside a practice of religious devotion. Once one has ceased to practise a religion, its externalized doctrinal justifications will seem hollow. Newman's religion was always personal. He spoke directly to God in prayer and he believed that God spoke to him. He travelled a very long way, and at great personal sacrifice, from the moment he gave his life to God at the age of fifteen, but on one level he was always the same person. It was appropriate that, when his greatness was finally recognized, and he was given a Cardinal's hat, Newman should have chosen as a motto on his coat of arms, *Cor ad cor loquitur,* Heart speaks to heart. For that is the essence of his religion.

Since boyhood, he had never been alone. Like the Psalmist, he had always been aware of a Presence beside him, and his loyalty and devotion to this Presence was unflinching.

It is this inner Newman whom I have tried to represent in this selection from his writings. Over the last few years I have re-read much of what he wrote, and I would confess that it has been a largely disillusioning experience. Dead ecclesiastical controversies are about as dead as anything, and so much of Newman's energy and writing was devoted to a consideration of these matters. The Irish bishoprics and the Jerusalem bishopric were the big questions in his Anglican days. In his Catholic days, he had to worry himself about such matters as whether the Archbishop of Dublin or the Archbishop of West-minster approved of him. Bishops, happily, like dreams, have a way of fleeing at the opening day. Matters which seem of overwhelming importance to institutional Christianity in one generation become, within a few decades, a matter of dead history. So it will be with the great issues with which churchmen fill their heads today. Yet, mysteriously, 'the voice of prayer is never silent'.

Newman has been hailed as a great prophet of twentieth-century Christianity. He has been seen, variously, as a proto-modernist, a father of the Second Vatican council, and he remains an inspiration to those who would prefer to think of themselves as 'traditional' Catholics. He has been seen, paradoxically but not unjustly, as a herald of ecumenism, and he is as much loved today in the Church which he left as in the Church he joined. I am not enough of a theologian to understand any of this. For most people in the English-speaking world, he is remembered as a poet – the man who wrote *The Dream of Gerontius*, with its most famous chorus ('Praise to the holiest in the height'), and as the author of one of the best-loved hymns, 'Lead, kindly light':

> The night is dark, and I am far from home –
> Lead thou me on!

There is something there to which many of us, uninterested in church politics, continue to respond.

A. N. Wilson
March 1989

Firmly I Believe

THE CALL OF FAITH

Faith is a Gift

To Mrs William Froude

If you saw more of me, you would not fancy I entertain such hard thoughts about people out of the Church, as you seem to do. Don't you know the distinction we make between formal and material error?

I am quite sure you wish to please God, and would do any thing He told you. On the other hand, I know well He does not tell us everything at once – but first one thing, and then, when we act upon that, another. No one ought to enter the Church without faith – no one can have faith for it by wishing or willing it, at the moment. Faith is a Gift of God; we can gain it by prayer, we cannot gain it at once; but we can gain it at last. I will quarrel with no one simply for not entering into the holiest and happiest of states on the spur of the instant – faith must be preceded by reason – but I will quarrel with him much, if he does not earnestly and continually ask of God the illumination which leads reason to faith.

Original Sin

If I looked into a mirror, and did not see my face, I should have the sort of feeling which actually comes upon me, when I look into this living busy world, and see no reflection of its Creator . . . Were it not for this voice, speaking so clearly in my conscience and my heart, I should be an atheist, or a pantheist, or a polytheist when I looked into the world . . . The sight of the world is nothing else than the prophet's scroll, full of 'lamentations, and mourning, and woe'.

To consider the world in its length and breadth, its various history, the many races of man, their starts, their fortunes, their mutual alienation, their conflicts; and then their ways, habits, governments, forms of worship; their enterprises, their aimless courses, their random achievements and acquirements, the impotent conclusion of long-standing facts, the tokens so faint and broken of a superintending design, the blind evolution of what turn out to be great powers or truths, the progress of things, as if from unreasoning elements, not towards final causes, the greatness and littleness of man, his far-reaching aims, his short duration, the curtain hung over his futurity, the disappointments of life, the defeat of good, the success of evil, physical pain, mental anguish, the prevalence and intensity of sin, the pervading idolatries, the corruptions, the dreary hopeless irreligion, that condition of the whole race, so fearfully yet exactly described in the Apostle's words, 'having no hope and without God in the world.' . . .

What shall be said to this heart-piercing, reason-bewildering fact? I can only answer, that either there is no Creator, or this living society of men is in a true sense discarded from His presence . . . *If* there be a God, *since* there is a God, the human race is implicated in some terrible aboriginal calamity. It is out of joint with the purposes of its Creator. This is a fact, a fact as true as the fact of its existence; and thus the doctrine of what is theologically called original sin becomes to me almost as certain as that the world exists, and as the existence of God.

———

The Voice of God

When the Divine Voice quickens us from the dust in which we lie, it is to call us to a dignity higher even than that which was ours in the beginning; but it restores us by degrees. At first, we emerge from the state of slaves into that of children and of children only, and not yet of men. We are exercised by faith; it is our education. And in like manner children are exercised at school; they are taught the rudiments of knowledge upon faith; they do not begin with philosophy. But, as in the natural order, we mount up to philosophical largeness of mind from lessons learned by rote and the schoolmaster's rod, so too in the order supernatural, even in this life, and far more truly in the life to come, we pass on from faith and penance to contemplation. Such is the loving-kindness of the Everlasting Father, *'suscitans a terra inopem, et de stercore erigens pauperem'*. To those who have begun with faith, He adds, in course of time, a higher gift, the gift of Wisdom, which, not superseding, but presupposing Faith, gives us so broad and deep a view of things revealed, that their very consistency is an evidence of their Author, and, like the visible world, persuades us to adore His Majesty.

Self-knowledge

Unless we have some just idea of our hearts and of sin, we can have no right idea of a Moral Governor, a Saviour or a Sanctifier . . . Thus self-knowledge is at the root of all real religious knowledge; and it is in vain – worse than vain – it is a deceit and a mischief, to think to understand the Christian doctrines as a matter of course, merely by being taught by books, or by attending sermons, or by any outward means, however excellent, taken by themselves. For it is in proportion as we search our hearts and understand our own nature, that we understand what is meant by an Infinite Governor and Judge; in proportion as we comprehend the nature of disobedience and our actual sinfulness, that we feel what is the blessing of the removal of sin, redemption, pardon, sanctification, which otherwise are mere words. God speaks to us primarily in our hearts. Self-knowledge is the key to the precepts and doctrines of Scripture. The very utmost any outward notices of religion can do, is to startle us and make us turn inward and search our hearts; and then, when we have experienced what it is to read ourselves, we shall profit by the doctrines of the Church and the Bible.

Believing

I am a Catholic by virtue of my believing in a God; and if I am asked why I believe in a God, I answer that it is because I believe in myself, for I feel it impossible to believe in my own existence (and of that fact I am quite sure) without believing also in the existence of Him, who lives as a Personal, All-seeing, All-judging Being in my conscience.

Knowledge of God

Is not the being of a God reported to us by testimony, handed down by history, inferred by an inductive process, brought home to us by metaphysical necessity, urged on us by the suggestions of our conscience? It is a truth in the natural order as well as in the supernatural. So much for its origin; and, when obtained, what is it worth? Is it a great truth or a small one? Is it a comprehensive truth? Say that no other religious idea whatever were given but it, and you have enough to fill the mind; you have at once a whole dogmatic system. The word 'God' is a theology in itself, indivisibly one, inexhaustibly various, from the vastness and the simplicity of its meaning. Admit a God, and you introduce among the subjects of your knowledge a fact encompassing, closing in upon, absorbing, every other fact conceivable. How can we investigate any part of any order of knowledge, and stop short of that which enters into every order? All true principles run over with it, all phenomena converge to it; it is truly the first and the last. In word indeed, and in idea, it is easy enough to divide knowledge into human and divine, secular and religious, and to lay down that we will address ourselves to the one without interfering with the other; but it is impossible in fact. Granting that divine truth differs in kind from human, so do human truths differ in kind one from another. If the knowledge of the Creator is in a different order from knowledge of the creature, so, in like manner, metaphysical science is in a different order from physical, physics from history, history from ethics. You will soon break up into fragments the whole circle of secular knowledge if you begin the mutilation with divine.

Looking up to God

A religious mind is ever marvelling, and irreligious men laugh and scoff at it because it marvels. A religious mind is ever looking out of itself, is ever pondering God's words, is ever 'looking into' them with the Angels, is ever realizing to itself Him on whom it depends, and who is the centre of all truth and good. Carnal and proud minds are contented with self; they like to remain at home; when they hear of mysteries, they have no devout curiosity to go and see the great sight, though it be ever so little out of their way; and when it actually falls in their path, they stumble at it. As great then as is the difference between hanging upon the thought of God and resting in ourselves, lifting up the heart to God and bringing all things in heaven and earth down to ourselves, exalting God and exalting reason, measuring things by God's power and measuring them by our own ignorance, so great is the difference between him who believes in the Christian mysteries and him who does not. And were there no other reason for the revelation of them but this gracious one, of raising us, refining us, making us reverent, making us expectant and devout, surely this would be more than a sufficient one.

The King of Creation

The laws of the universe, the principles of truth, the relation of one thing to another, their qualities and virtues, the order and harmony of the whole, all that exists, is from Him; and, if evil is not from Him, as assuredly it is not, this is because evil has no substance of its own, but is only the defect, excess, perversion, or corruption of that which has. All we see, hear, and touch, the remote sidereal firmament, as well as our own sea and land, and the elements which compose them, and the ordinances they obey, are His. The primary atoms of matter, their properties, their mutual action, their disposition and collocation, electricity, magnetism, gravitation, light, and whatever other subtle principles or operations the wit of man is detecting or shall detect, are the works of His hands. From Him has been every movement which has convulsed and refashioned the surface of the earth. The most insignificant or unsightly insect, is from Him, and good in its kind; the ever-teeming, inexhaustible swarms of animalculæ, the myriads of living motes invisible to the naked eye, the restless everspreading vegetation which creeps like a garment over the whole earth, the lofty cedar, the umbrageous banana, are His. His are the tribes and families of birds and beasts, their graceful forms, their wild gestures, and their passionate cries.

And so in the intellectual, moral, social, and political world. Man, with his motives and works, his languages, his propagation, his diffusion, is from Him. Agriculture, medicine, and the arts of life, are His gifts. Society, laws, government, He is their sanction. The pageant of earthly royalty has the semblance and the benediction of the Eternal King. Peace and civilization, commerce and adventure, wars when just, conquest when humane and necessary, have His co-operation, and His blessing upon them. The course of events, the revolution of Empires, the rise and fall of states, the periods and eras, the progresses and the retrogressions of the world's history, not indeed the incidental sin, over-abundant as it is, but the great outlines and issues of human affairs, are from His disposition.

All that is Good

The old saws of nations, the majestic precepts of philosophy, the luminous maxims of law, the oracles of individual wisdom, the traditionary rules of truth, justice, and religion, even though imbedded in the corruption, or alloyed with the pride, of the world, bespeak His original agency, and His long-suffering presence. Even where there is habitual rebellion against Him, or profound far-speading social depravity, still the undercurrent, or the heroic outburst, of natural virtue, as well as the yearnings of the heart after what it has not, and its presentiment of its true remedies, are to be ascribed to the Author of all good. Anticipations or reminiscences of His glory haunt the mind of the self-sufficient sage, and of the pagan devotee; His writing is upon the wall, whether of the Indian fane, or of the porticoes of Greece. He introduces, He all but concurs, according to His good pleasure, and in His selected season, in the issues of unbelief, superstition, and false worship, and changes the character of acts, by His over-ruling operation. He condescends, though He gives no sanction, to the altars and shrines of imposture, and He makes His own fiat the substitute for its sorceries. He speaks amid the incantations of Balaam, raises Samuel's spirit in the witch's cavern, prophesies of the Messias by the tongue of the Sibyl, forces Python to recognize His ministers, and baptizes by the hand of the misbeliever. He is with the heathen dramatist in his denunciations of injustice and tyranny, and his auguries of divine vengeance upon crime. Even on the unseemly legends of a popular mythology He casts His shadow, and is dimly discerned in the ode or the epic, as in troubled water or in fantastic dreams. All that is good, all that is true, all that is beautiful, all that is beneficent, be it great or small, be it perfect or fragmentary, natural as well as supernatural, moral as well as material, comes from Him.

Where is Truth?

God who made the Prophet's ass speak, and thereby instructed the Prophet, might instruct His Church by means of heathen Babylon . . .

It does not therefore seem to me difficult, nay, nor even unlikely, that the prophets of Israel should, in the course of God's providence, have gained new truths from the heathen, among whom those truths lay corrupted. The Church of God in every age has been, as it were, on visitation through the earth, surveying, judging, sifting, selecting, and refining all matters of thought and practice; detecting what was precious amid what is ruined and refuse, and putting her seal upon it.

Truth is Sacred

Is not this the error, the common and fatal error, of the world, to think itself a judge of Religious Truth without preparation of heart? 'I am the good Shepherd, and know My sheep, and am known of Mine.' 'He goeth before them, and the sheep follow Him, for they know His voice.' 'The pure in heart shall see God'; 'to the meek mysteries are revealed'; 'he that is spiritual judgeth all things.' 'The darkness comprehendeth it not.' Gross eyes see not; heavy ears hear not. But in the schools of the world the ways towards Truth are considered high roads open to all men, however disposed, at all times. Truth is to be approached without homage. Everyone is considered on a level with his neighbour; or rather the powers of the intellect, acuteness, sagacity, subtleness, and depth, are thought the guides into Truth. Men consider that they have as full a right to discuss religious subjects, as if they were themselves religious. They will enter upon the most sacred points of Faith at the moment, at their pleasure – if it so happen, in a careless frame of mind, in their hours of recreation, over the wine cup. Is it wonderful that they so frequently end in becoming indifferentists, and conclude that Religious Truth is but a name, that all men are right and all wrong, from witnessing externally the multitude of sects and parties, and from the clear consciousness they possess within, that their own inquiries end in darkness?

Illusions of Unbelief

The first time the mind comes across the arguments and speculations of unbelievers, and feels what a novel light they cast upon what he has hitherto accounted sacred; and still more, if it gives in to them and embraces them, and throws off as so much prejudice what it has hitherto held, and, as if waking from a dream, begins to realize to its imagination that there is now no such thing as law and the transgression of law, that sin is a phantom, and punishment a bugbear, that it is free to sin, free to enjoy the world and the flesh; and still further, when it does enjoy them, and reflects that it may think and hold just what it will, that 'the world is all before it where to choose', and what system to build up as its own private persuasion; when this torrent of wilful thoughts rushes over and inundates it, who will deny that the fruit of the tree of knowledge, or what the mind takes for knowledge, has made it one of the gods, with a sense of expansion and elevation, an intoxication in reality, still, so far as the subjective state of the mind goes, an illumination? Hence the fanaticism of individuals or nations who suddenly cast off their Maker. Their eyes are opened; and, like the judgement-stricken king in the tragedy, they see two suns, and a magic universe, out of which they look back upon their former state of faith and innocence with a sort of contempt and indignation, as if they were then but fools, and the dupes of imposture.

On the other hand, religion has its own enlargement, and an enlargement, not of tumult, but of peace. It is often remarked of uneducated persons, who have hitherto thought little of the unseen world, that, on their turning to God, looking into themselves, regulating their hearts, reforming their conduct, and meditating on death and judgement, heaven and hell, they seem to become, in point of intellect, different beings from what they were. Before, they took things as they came, and thought no more of one thing than another. But now every event has a meaning; they have their own estimate of whatever happens to them; they are mindful of times and seasons, and compare the present with the past; and the world, no longer dull, monotonous, unprofitable, and hopeless, is a various and complicated drama, with parts and an object, and an awful moral.

Beyond Rationalism

Faith is, in its very nature, the acceptance of what our reason cannot reach, simply and absolutely upon testimony.

There is, of course, a multitude of cases in which we allowably and rightly accept statements as true, partly on reason, and partly on testimony. We supplement the information of others by our own knowledge, by our own judgement of probabilities; and, if it be very strange and extravagant, we suspend our assent. This is undeniable; still, after all, there are truths which are incapable of reaching us except on testimony, and there is testimony which, by and in itself, has an imperative claim on our acceptance.

As regards Revealed Truth, it is not Rationalism to set about to ascertain, by the exercise of reason, what things are attainable by reason, and what are not; nor, in the absence of an express Revelation, to inquire into the truths of Religion, as they come to us by nature; nor to determine what proofs are necessary for the acceptance of a Revelation, if it be given; nor to reject a Revelation on the plea of insufficient proof; nor, after recognizing it as divine, to investigate the meaning of its declarations, and to interpret its language; nor to use its doctrines, as far as they can be fairly used, in inquiring into its divinity; nor to compare and connect them with our previous knowledge, with a view of making them parts of a whole; nor to bring them into dependence on each other, to trace their mutual relations, and to pursue them to their legitimate issues. This is not Rationalism; but it is Rationalism to accept the Revelation, and then to explain it away; to speak of it as the Word of God, and to treat it as the word of man; to refuse to let it speak for itself; to claim to be told the *why* and the *how* of God's dealings with us, as therein described, and to assign to Him a motive and a scope of our own; to stumble at the partial knowledge which He may give us of them; to put aside what is obscure, as if it had not been said at all; to accept one half of what has been told us, and not the other half; to assume that the contents of Revelation are also its proof; to frame some gratuitous hypothesis about them, and then to garble, gloss and colour them, to trim, clip, and pare away, and twist them, in order to bring them into conformity with the idea to which we have subjected them . . .

The Rationalist makes himself his own centre, not His Maker; he does not go to God, but he implies that God must come to him.

[15]

The Scientific Imagination

To W. S. Lilly

First, we must grant – and it is difficult to determine how far we must go in granting – that both the Mosaic and Christian dispensations took the existing state of thought as it was, and only partially innovated on and corrected it. The instance of Divorce makes this plain as regards the Old Testament; as to the New, the first instance that occurs to me is St Paul's simple recognition of married life in Bishops.

On a far larger scale is the absence of meddling with the social and secular world. God speaks 'for the elect's sake'. He leaves the popular astronomy as it was. Heaven is still above, and the powers of evil below. The sun rises and sets, and at His word stops or goes back, and the firmament opens. And so with social and political science; nothing is told us of economical laws, etc. So from the first there has been a progress with laws of progress, to which theology has contributed little, and which now has a form and substance, powerful in itself, and independent of and far surpassing Christianity in its social aspect; for Christianity (socially considered) has a previous and more elementary office, being the binding principle of society.

This primary and special office of religion men of the world do not see, and they see only its poverty as a principle of secular progress, and, as disciples and upholders and servants of that great scientific progress, they look on religion and despise it. As the scientific parasite says in the play, *'Ego illum contempsi prae me'* [Terence, *Eunuchus* II, ii, 8].

I consider then that it is not reason that is against us, but imagination. The mind, after having, to the utter neglect of the Gospels, lived in science, experiences, on coming back to Scripture, an utter strangeness in what it reads, which seems to it a better argument against Revelation than any formal proof from definite facts or logical statements. 'Christianity is behind the age.'

___

Morality and Revelation

To H. A. Woodgate

Why do men *agree* to say this deed is right, that man is good, that maxim is praiseworthy? *Why* is there a 'consensus'? *How* comes it about? The *reason why* they agree is the *proper* definition of right, goodness, truth and beautifulness, not the mere fact of their agreeing. They agree, because there is an objective right, goodness, etc., which they mentally see – that objective right etc. is the *moral* law – and if I am asked where the moral law is, I answer, that it is realized in God. What all men dimly see, one and all, and therefore they agree in, is the shadow of the divine attributes.

These moral truths are eternal – according to the lines in the *Antigone* – and very different from the facts of Revelation (even though some of *them* are eternal too). Christians agree in Christian doctrine, *not* because it is *eternal* and the object of their *moral sense*, but because it is actually *revealed*, and handed down to them by *tradition*. 'Consent' is the convenient witness and test *both* of moral truth *and* of revealed – but of moral, because it is seen and approved by the mind naturally; of revealed because it has been handed down by the Church to her children.

It is usual in theology to say that the most authoritative and august proof of the Being of a God is the visible world – (according to Rom. 1, 20) yet in matter of fact children are taught (1) by their *parents*, and next (2) (as I have drawn out in my Essay on Assent) by their *conscience*. That is, in the *ordo logicus* the argument for Theism from creation comes first; but in the *ordo chronologicus* the arguments from authority and conscience come first. In like manner in gaining moral truth chrono-logically, historically, actually, personally *'consensus'* may come first – but logically and philosophically *the moral sense*.

There are two kinds of truth, that which we know intuitively and that which we know by revelation. The latter from the nature of the case comes to us from without; the former primarily comes to us from within.

Natural Conscience

Conscience is a connecting principle between the creature and his Creator; and the firmest hold of theological truths is gained by habits of personal religion. When men begin all their works with the thought of God, acting for His sake, and to fulfil His will, when they ask His blessing on themselves and their life, pray to Him for the objects they desire, and see Him in the event, whether it be according to their prayers or not, they will find everything that happens tend to confirm them in the truths about Him which live in their imagination, varied and unearthly as those truths may be. Then they are brought into His presence as that of a Living Person, and are able to hold converse with Him, and that with a directness and simplicity, with a confidence and intimacy, *mutatis mutandis*, which we use towards an earthly superior; so that it is doubtful whether we realize the company of our fellow-men with greater keenness than these favoured minds are able to contemplate and adore the Unseen, Incomprehensible Creator.

This vivid apprehension of religious objects, on which I have been enlarging, is independent of the written records of Revelation; it does not require any knowledge of Scripture, nor of the history or the teaching of the Catholic Church. It is independent of books . . .

To a mind thus carefully formed upon the basis of its natural conscience, the world, both of nature and of man, does but give back a reflection of those truths about the One Living God, which have been familiar to it from childhood.

We Know in Part

The question is whether a real assent to the mystery, as such, is possible; and I say it is not possible, because, though we can image the separate propositions, we cannot image them altogether. We cannot, because the mystery transcends all our experience; we have no experiences in our memory which we can put together, compare, contrast, unite, and thereby transmute into an image of the Ineffable Verity – certainly; but what *is* in some degree a matter of experience, what *is* presented for the imagination, the affections, the devotion, the spiritual life of the Christian to repose upon with a real assent, what stands for things, not for notions only, is each of those propositions taken one by one, and that, not in the case of intellectual and thoughtful minds only, but of all religious minds whatever, in the case of a child or a peasant, as well as of a philosopher.

This is only one instance of a general principle which holds good in all such real apprehension as is possible to us, of God and His Attributes. Not only do we see Him at best only in shadows, but we cannot bring even those shadows together, for they flit to and fro, and are never present to us at once. We can indeed combine the various matters which we know of Him by an act of the intellect, and treat them theologically, but such theological combinations are no objects for the imagination to gaze upon. Our image of Him never is one, but broken into numberless partial aspects, independent each of each. As we cannot see the whole starry firmament at once, but have to turn ourselves from east to west, and then round to east again, sighting first one constellation and then another, and losing these in order to gain those, so it is, and much more, with such real apprehensions as we can secure of the Divine Nature. We know one truth about Him and another truth – but we cannot image both of them together; we cannot bring them before us by one act of the mind; we drop the one while we turn to take up the other.

Faith and Doubt

Thus we may wonder at the Divine Mercy of the Incarnation, till we grow startled at it, and ask why the earth has so special a theological history, or why we are Christians and others not, or how God can really exert a particular governance, since He does not punish such sinners as we are, thus seeming to doubt His power or His equity, though in truth we are not doubting at all.

The occasion of this intellectual waywardness may be slighter still. I gaze on the Palatine Hill, or on the Parthenon, or on the Pyramids, which I have read of from a boy, or upon the matter-of-fact reality of the sacred places in the Holy Land, and I have to force my imagination to follow the guidance of sight and of reason. It is to me so strange that a lifelong belief should be changed into sight, and things should be so near me, which hitherto had been visions. And so in times, first of suspense, then of joy; 'When the Lord turned the captivity of Sion, then' (according to the Hebrew text) 'we were like unto them that dream.' Yet it was a dream which they were certain was a truth, while they seemed to doubt it. So, too, was it in some sense with the Apostles after our Lord's resurrection.

Such vague thoughts, haunting or evanescent, are in no sense akin to that struggle between faith and unbelief, which made the poor father cry out, 'I believe, help Thou mine unbelief!' Nay, even what in some minds seems like an undercurrent of scepticism, or a faith founded on a perilous substratum of doubt, need not be more than a temptation, though robbing Certitude of its normal peacefulness. In such a case, faith may still express the steady conviction of the intellect; it may still be the grave, deep, calm, prudent assurance of mature experience, though it is not the ready and impetuous assent of the young, the generous, or the unreflecting.

The Victory of Faith

We are in a world of mystery, with one bright Light before us, sufficient for our proceeding forward through all difficulties. Take away this Light and we are utterly wretched – we know not where we are, how we are sustained, what will become of us, and of all that is dear to us, what we are to believe, and why we are in being. But with it we have all and abound. Not to mention the duty and wisdom of implicit faith in the love of Him who made and redeemed us, what is nobler, what is more elevating and transporting, than the generosity of heart which risks everything on God's word, dares the powers of evil to their worst efforts, and repels the illusions of sense and the artifices of reason, by confidence in the Truth of Him who has ascended to the right hand of the Majesty on high? What infinite mercy it is in Him, that He allows sinners such as we are, the privilege of acting the part of heroes rather than of penitents. Who are we 'that we should be able' and have opportunity 'to offer so willingly after this sort?' – 'Blessed,' surely thrice blessed, 'are they who have not seen, and yet have believed!' We will not wish for sight; we will enjoy our privilege; we will triumph in the leave given us to go forward, 'not knowing whither we go,' knowing that 'this is the victory that overcometh the world, even our faith.'

Seeing Afterwards

He said to St Peter, 'What I do, thou knowest not now, but thou shalt know hereafter.' Again, 'These things understood not His disciples at the first, but when Jesus was glorified, then remembered they that these things were written of Him, and that they had done these things unto Him.'

And in like manner while He talked with the two disciples going to Emmaus, their eyes were holden that they did not know Him. When they recognized Him, at once He vanished out of their sight. *Then* 'they said one to another, Did not our heart burn within us, while He talked with us by the way?' (Luke 24.32) . . .

Such is God's rule in Scripture, to dispense His blessings silently and secretly; so that we do not discern them at the time, except by faith, afterwards only . . .

Thus the presence of God is like His glory as it appeared to Moses; He said, 'Thou canst not see My face . . . and live;' but He passed by, and Moses saw that glory behind, which he might not see in front, or in passing; he saw it as it retired, and he acknowledged it, and 'made haste and bowed his head toward the earth, and worshipped.'

Now consider how parallel this is to what takes place in the providences of daily life. Events happen to us pleasant or painful; we do not know at the time the meaning of them, we do not see God's hand in them. If indeed we have faith, we confess what we do not see, and take all that happens as His; but whether we will accept it in faith or not, certainly there is no other way of accepting it . . .

And so, again, in a number of other occurrences, not striking, not grievous, not pleasant, but ordinary, we are able afterwards to discern that He has been with us, and, like Moses, to worship Him. Let a person, who trusts he is on the whole serving God acceptably, look back upon his past life, and he will find how critical were moments and acts, which at the time seemed the most indifferent: as, for instance, the school he was sent to as a child, the occasion of his falling in with those persons who have most benefited him, the accidents which determined his calling or prospects, whatever they were. God's hand is ever over his own, and He leads them forward by a way they know not of.

Living in the Presence of Christ

True faith is what may be called colourless, like air or water; it is but the medium through which the soul sees Christ; and the soul as little really rests upon it and contemplates it as the eye can see the air . . . As God's grace elicits our faith, so His holiness stirs our fear, and His glory kindles our love. Others may say of us 'here is faith', and 'there is conscientiousness', and 'there is love'; but we can only say 'this is God's grace', and 'that is His holiness', and 'that is His glory'.

And this being the difference between true faith and self-contemplation, no wonder that where the thought of self obscures the thought of God, prayer and praise languish, and only preaching flourishes. Divine worship is simply contemplating our Maker, Redeemer, Sanctifier, and Judge; but discoursing, conversing, making speeches, arguing, reading, and writing about religion, tend to make us forget Him in ourselves. The Ancients worshipped; they went out of their own minds into the Infinite Temple which was around them. They saw Christ in the Gospels, in the Creed, in the Sacraments and other Rites; in the visible structure and ornaments of His House, in the Altar, and in the Cross; and, not content with giving the service of their eyes, they gave Him their voices, their bodies, and their time, gave up their rest by night and their leisure by day, all that could evidence the offering of their hearts to Him . . . Unwavering, unflagging, not urged by fits and starts, not heralding forth their feelings, but resolutely, simply, perseveringly, day after day, Sunday and week-day, fast-day and festival, week by week, season by season, year by year, in youth and in age, through a life, thirty years, forty years, fifty years, in prelude of the everlasting chant before the Throne – so they went on 'continuing *instant* in prayer', after the pattern of Psalmists and Apostles, in the day with David, in the night with Paul and Silas, winter and summer, in heat and in cold, in peace and in danger, in a prison or in a cathedral, in the dark, in the day-break, at sun-rising, in the forenoon, at noon, in the afternoon, at eventide, and on going to rest, still they had Christ before them; His thought in their mind, His emblems in their eye, His name in their mouth, His service in their posture, magnifying Him, and calling on all that lives to magnify Him, joining with Angels in heaven and Saints in Paradise to bless and praise Him for ever and ever . . .

[23]

Communion with God

There is another reason why God alone is the happiness of our souls, to which I wish to direct attention. The contemplation of Him, and nothing but it, is able fully to open and relieve the mind, to unlock, occupy, and fix our affections. We may indeed love things created with great intenseness, but such affection, when disjoined from the love of the Creator, is like a stream running in a narrow channel, impetuous, vehement, turbid. The heart runs out, as it were, only at one door; it is not an expanding of the whole man. Created natures cannot open us, or elicit the ten thousand mental senses which belong to us, and through which we really live. None but the presence of our Maker can enter us; for to none besides can the whole heart in all its thoughts and feelings be unlocked and subjected. 'Behold', He says, 'I stand at the door and knock; if any man hear My voice and open the door, I will come in to him, and will sup with him, and he with Me.' 'My Father will love him, and We will come unto him, and make Our abode with him.' 'God hath sent forth the Spirit of His Son into your hearts.' 'God is greater than our heart, and knoweth all things.' It is this feeling of simple and absolute confidence and communion which soothes and satisfies those to whom it is vouchsafed.

_____

God Alone is True

We know that even our nearest friends enter into us but partially, and hold intercourse with us only at times; whereas the consciousness of a perfect and enduring Presence, and it alone, keeps the heart open. Withdraw the Object on which it rests, and it will relapse again into its state of confinement and constraint; and in proportion as it is limited, either to certain seasons or to certain affections, the heart is straitened and distressed. If it be not overbold to say it, He who is infinite can alone be its measure; He alone can answer to the mysterious assemblage of feelings and thoughts which it has within it . . .

Life passes, riches fly away, popularity is fickle, the senses decay, the world changes, friends die. One alone is constant; One alone is true to us; One alone can be true; One alone can be all things to us; One alone can supply our needs; One alone can train us up to our full perfection; One alone can give a meaning to our complex and intricate nature; One alone can give us tune and harmony; One alone can form and possess us.

Absolute Trust

God has created me to do Him some definite service; He has committed some work to me which He has not committed to another. I have my mission – I never may know it in this life, but I shall be told it in the next . . . I have a part in a great work; I am a link in a chain, a bond of connection between persons. He has not created me for naught. I shall do good, I shall do His work; I shall be an angel of peace, a preacher of truth in my own place, while not intending it, if I do but keep His commandments and serve Him in my calling.

Therefore I will trust Him. Whatever, wherever I am, I can never be thrown away. If I am in sickness, my sickness may serve Him; in perplexity, my perplexity may serve Him; if I am in sorrow, my sorrow may serve Him. My sickness, or perplexity, or sorrow may be necessary causes of some great end, which is quite beyond us. He does nothing in vain; He may prolong my life, He may shorten it; He knows what He is about. He may take away my friends, He may throw me among strangers, He may make me feel desolate, make my spirits sink, hide the future from me – still He knows what He is about.

Power in Weakness

Those men are not necessarily the most useful men in their generation, nor the most favoured by God, who make the most noise in the world, and who seem to be principals in the great changes and events recorded in history; on the contrary, even when we are able to point to a certain number of men as the real instruments of any great blessings vouchsafed to mankind, our relative estimate of them, one with another, is often very erroneous: so that on the whole, if we would trace truly the hand of God in human affairs, and pursue His bounty as displayed in the world to its original sources, we must unlearn our reliance on the opinion of society, our respect for the decisions of the learned or the multitude, and turn our eyes to private life, watching in all we read or witness for the true signs of God's presence, the graces of personal holiness manifested in His elect; which, weak as they may seem to mankind, are mighty through God, and have an influence upon the course of His Providence, and bring about great events in the world at large, when the wisdom and strength of the natural man are of no avail.

A Stern Necessity

To Mrs J. Mozley

How life is going! I see men dying who were boys, almost children, when I was born. Pass a very few years, and I am an old man. What means of judging can I have more than I have? What maturity of mind am I to expect? If I am right to move at all, surely it is high time not to delay about it longer. Let me give my strength to the work, not my weakness – years in which I can profit the cause which calls me, not the dregs of life. Is it not like a death-bed repentance to put off what one feels one ought to do?

As to my convictions, I can but say what I have told you already, that I cannot at all make out *why* I should determine on moving, except as thinking I should offend God by not doing so. I cannot make out what I am *at* except on this supposition. At my time of life men love ease. I love ease myself. I am giving up a maintenance involving no duties, and adequate to all my wants. What in the world am I doing this for (I ask *myself* this), except that I think I am called to do so? I am making a large income by my sermons. I am, to say the very least, risking this; the chance is that my sermons will have no further sale at all. I have a good name with many; I am deliberately sacrificing it. I have a bad name with more; I am fulfilling all their worst wishes, and giving them their most coveted triumph. I am distressing all I love, unsettling all I have instructed or aided. I am going to those whom I do not know, and of whom I expect very little. I am making myself an outcast, and that at my age. Oh, what can it be but a stern necessity which causes this?

We are not Our Own

We are not our own, any more than what we possess is our own. We did not make ourselves; we cannot be supreme over ourselves. We cannot be our own masters. We are God's property by creation, by redemption, by regeneration. He has a triple claim upon us. Is it not our happiness thus to view the matter? Is it any happiness, or any comfort, to consider that we *are* our own? It may be thought so by the young and prosperous. These may think it a great thing to have everything, as they suppose, their own way – to depend on no one – to have to think of nothing out of sight – to be without the irksomeness of continual acknowledgement, continual prayer, continual reference of what they do to the will of another. But as time goes on, they, as all men, will find that independence was not made for man – that it is an unnatural state – may do for a while, but will not carry us on safely to the end. No, we are creatures; and, as being such, we have two duties, to be resigned and to be thankful.

Let us then view God's providences towards us more religiously than we have hitherto done. Let us try to gain a truer view of what we are, and where we are, in His kingdom. Let us humbly and reverently attempt to trace His guiding hand in the years which we have hitherto lived. Let us thankfully commemorate the many mercies He has vouchsafed to us in time past, the many sins He has not remembered, the many dangers He has averted, the many prayers He has answered, the many mistakes He has corrected, the many warnings, the many lessons, the much light, the abounding comfort which He has from time to time given. Let us dwell upon times and seasons, times of trouble, times of joy, times of trial, times of refreshment. How did He cherish us as children! How did He guide us in that dangerous time when the mind began to think for itself, and the heart to open to the world! How did He with His sweet discipline restrain our passions, mortify our hopes, calm our fears, enliven our heavinesses, sweeten our desolateness, and strengthen our infirmities! How did He gently guide us towards the strait gate! How did He allure us along His everlasting way, in spite of its strictness, in spite of its loneliness, in spite of the dim twilight in which it lay! He has been all things to us.

Faith in the Church

Trust the Church of God implicitly, even when your natural judgement would take a different course from hers, and would induce you to question her prudence or her correctness. Recollect what a hard task she has; how she is sure to be criticized and spoken against, whatever she does; recollect how much she needs your loyal and tender devotion. Recollect, too, how long is the experience gained in eighteen hundred years, and what a right she has to claim your assent to principles which have had so extended and so triumphant a trial. Thank her that she has kept the faith safe for so many generations, and do your part in helping her to transmit it to generations after you.

Faith in the Creeds

Break a ray of light into its constituent colours, each is beautiful, each may be enjoyed; attempt to unite them, and perhaps you produce only a dirty white. The pure and indivisible Light is seen only by the blessed inhabitants of heaven; here we have but such faint reflections of it as its diffraction supplies; but they are sufficient for faith and devotion. Attempt to combine them into one, and you gain nothing but a mystery, which you can describe as a notion, but cannot depict as an imagination. And this, which holds of the Divine Attributes, holds also of the Holy Trinity in Unity. And hence, perhaps, it is that the latter doctrine is never spoken of as a Mystery in the sacred book, which is addressed far more to the imagination and affections than to the intellect. Hence, too, what is more remarkable, in the Creeds the dogma is not called a mystery; not in the Apostles' nor the Nicene, nor even in the Athanasian. The reason seems to be, that the Creeds have a place in the Ritual; they are devotional acts, and of the nature of prayers, addressed to God; and, in such addresses, to speak of intellectual difficulties would be out of place. It must be recollected especially that the Athanasian Creed has sometimes been called the 'Psalmus *Quicunque*'. It is not a mere collection of notions, however momentous. It is a psalm or hymn of praise, of confession, and of profound, self-prostrating homage, parallel to the canticles of the elect in the Apocalypse. It appeals to the imagination quite as much as to the intellect.

For myself, I have ever felt it as the most simple and sublime, the most devotional formulary to which Christianity has given birth, more so even than the *Veni Creator* and the *Te Deum*.

Firmly I Believe

Firmly I believe and truly
   God is three, and God is One;
And I next acknowledge duly
   Manhood taken by the Son.
And I trust and hope most fully
   In that Manhood crucified;
And each thought and deed unruly
   Do to death, as He has died.
Simply to His grace and wholly
   Light and life and strength belong,
And I love, supremely, solely,
   Him the holy, Him the strong.
Sanctus fortis, Sanctus Deus,
   De profundis oro te,
Miserere, Judex meus,
   Parce mihi, Domine.
And I hold in veneration,
   For the love of Him alone,
Holy Church, as His creation,
   And her teachings, as His own.
And I take with joy whatever
   Now besets me, pain or fear,
And with a strong will I sever
   All the ties which bind me here.

In my Innermost Heart

THE ART OF PRAYER

What is Prayer?

What, then is prayer? It is (if it may be said reverently) *conversing* with God. We converse with our fellow-men, and then we use familiar language, because they *are* our fellows. We converse with God, and then we use the lowliest, awfullest, calmest, concisest language we can, because He *is* God. Prayer, then, is *divine* converse, differing from human as God differs from man. Thus St Paul says, 'Our conversation is in heaven', not indeed thereby meaning converse of words only, but intercourse and manner of living generally; yet still in an especial way converse of words or prayer, because language is the special means of all intercourse. Our intercourse with our fellow-men goes on, not by sight, but by sound, not by eyes, but by ears. Hearing is the social sense, and language is the social bond. In like manner, as the Christian's conversation is in heaven, as it is his duty, with Enoch and other saints, *to walk with God*, so is his voice in heaven, his heart 'inditing of a good matter', of prayers and praises. Prayers and praises are the mode of his intercourse with the next world, as the converse of business or recreation is the mode in which this world is carried on in all its separate courses. He who does not pray does not claim his citizenship with heaven, but lives, though an heir of the kingdom, as if he were a child of earth.

Now, it is not surprising if that duty or privilege, which is the characteristic token of our heavenly inheritance, should also have an especial influence upon our fitness for claiming it. He who does not use a gift, loses it; the man who does not use his voice or limbs, loses power over them, and becomes disqualified for the state of life to which he is called. In like manner, he who neglects to pray, not only suspends the enjoyment, but is in a way to lose the possession, of his divine citizenship. We are members of another world; we have been severed from the companionship of devils, and brought into that invisible kingdom of Christ which faith alone discerns – that mysterious Presence of God which encompasses us, which is in us, and around us, which is in our heart, which enfolds us as though with a robe of light, hiding our scarred and discoloured souls from the sight of Divine Purity, and making them shining as the Angels . . .

Jesus the Light of the Soul

I adore Thee, O my God, as the true and only Light! From Eternity to Eternity, before any creature was, when Thou wast alone, alone but not solitary, for Thou hast ever been Three in One, Thou wast the Infinite Light. There was none to see Thee but Thyself. The Father saw that Light in the Son, and the Son in the Father. Such as Thou wast in the beginning, such Thou art now. Most separate from all creatures in this Thy uncreated brightness. Most glorious, most beautiful. Thy attributes are so many separate and resplendent colours, each as perfect in its own purity and grace as if it were the sole and highest perfection. Nothing created is more than the very shadow of Thee. Bright as are the Angels, they are poor and most unworthy shadows of Thee. They pale and look dim and gather blackness before Thee. They are so feeble beside Thee, that they are unable to gaze upon Thee. The highest Seraphim veil their eyes, by deed as well as by word proclaiming Thy unutterable glory. For me, I cannot even look upon the sun, and what is this but a base material emblem of Thee? How should I endure to look even on an Angel? and how could I look upon Thee and live? If I were placed in the illumination of Thy countenance, I should shrink up like the grass. O most gracious God, who shall approach Thee, being so glorious, yet how can I keep from Thee?

God is Holy

To rush into His presence, to address Him familiarly, to urge Him, to strive to make our duty lie in one direction when it lies in another, to handle rudely and practise upon His holy Word, to trifle with truth, to treat conscience lightly, to take liberties (as it may be called) with anything that is God's, all irreverence, profaneness, unscrupulousness, wantonness, is represented in Scripture not only as a sin, but as felt, noticed, quickly returned on God's part (if I may dare use such human words of the Almighty and All-holy God, without transgressing the rule I am myself laying down – but He vouchsafes in Scripture to represent Himself to us in that only way in which we can attain to the knowledge of Him), I say all irreverence towards God is represented as being jealously and instantly and fearfully noticed and visited, as friend or stranger among men might resent an insult shown him. This should be carefully considered; we are apt to act towards God and the things of God as towards a mere system, a law, a name, a religion, a principle, not as against a Person, a living, watchful, present, prompt, and powerful Eye and Arm.

———

What am I?

What communion then can there be between Thee and me? O my God! what am I but a parcel of dead bones, a feeble, tottering, miserable being, compared with Thee. I am Thy work, and Thou didst create me pure from sin, but how canst Thou look upon me, in my best estate of nature, with complacency? how canst Thou see in me any image of Thyself, the Creator? How is this, my Lord? Thou didst pronounce Thy work very good, and didst make man in Thy image. Yet there is an infinite gulf between Thee and me, O my God.

Always with God

Is God habitually in our thoughts? Do we think of Him, and of His Son our Saviour, through the day? When we eat and drink, do we thank Him, not as a mere matter of form, but in spirit? When we do things in themselves right, do we lift up our minds to Him, and desire to promote His glory? When we are in the exercise of our callings, do we still think of Him, acting ever conscientiously, desiring to know His will more exactly than we do at present, and aiming at fulfilling it more completely and abundantly? Do we wait on His grace to enlighten, renew, strengthen us?

I do not ask whether we use many words about religion. There is no need to do this: nay, we should avoid a boastful display of our better feelings and practices, silently serving God without human praise, and hiding our conscientiousness except when it would dishonour God to do so. There are times, indeed, when, in the presence of a holy man, to confess is a benefit, and there are times when, in the presence of worldly men, to confess becomes a duty; but these seasons, whether of privilege or of duty, are comparatively rare. But we are always with ourselves and our God; and that silent inward confession in His presence may be sustained and continual, and will end in durable fruit.

My Infinite Lord

My God, I believe and know and adore Thee as infinite in the multiplicity and depth of Thy attributes. I adore Thee as containing in Thee an abundance of all that can delight and satisfy the soul. I know, on the contrary, and from sad experience I am too sure, that whatever is created, whatever is earthly pleases but for the time, and then palls and is a weariness. I believe that there is nothing at all here below, which I should not at length get sick of. I believe, that, though I had all the means of happiness which this life could give, yet in time I should tire of living, feeling everything trite and dull and unprofitable. I believe, that, were it my lot to live the long antediluvian life, and to live it without Thee, I should be utterly, inconceivably, wretched at the end of it. I think I should be tempted to destroy myself for very weariness and disgust. I think I should at last lose my reason and go mad, if my life here was prolonged long enough. I should feel it like solitary confinement, for I should find myself shut up in myself without companion, if I could not converse with Thee, my God. Thou only, O my infinite Lord, art ever new, though Thou art the ancient of days – the last as well as the first.

Pray Always

To be religious is, in other words, to have the habit of prayer, or to pray always. This is what Scripture means by doing all things to God's glory; that is, so placing God's presence and will before us, and so consistently acting with a reference to Him, that all we do becomes one body and course of obedience, witnessing without ceasing to Him who made us, and whose servants we are; and in its separate parts promoting more or less directly His glory; according as each particular thing we happen to be doing admits more or less of a religious character. Thus religious obedience is, as it were, a spirit dwelling in us, extending its influence to every motion of the soul; and just as healthy men and strong men show their health and strength in all they do (not indeed equally in all things, but in some things more than in others, because all actions do not require or betoken the presence of that health and strength, and yet even in their step, and their voice, and their gestures, and their countenance, showing in due measure their vigour of body), so they who have the true health and strength of the soul, a clear, sober, and deep faith in Him in whom they have their being, will in all they do, nay (as St Paul says), even whether they 'eat or drink', be living in God's sight, or, in the words of the same Apostle in the text, live in ceaseless prayer . . . Our spiritual 'life' (as St Paul says) 'is *hid* with Christ in God'. But as our bodily life discovers itself by its activity, so is the presence of the Holy Spirit in us discovered by a spiritual activity; and this activity is the spirit of continual prayer. Prayer is to spiritual life what the beating of the pulse and the drawing of the breath are to the life of the body . . .

———

I Love to Think of Thee

Almighty God, Thou art the One Infinite Fullness. From eternity Thou art the One and only absolute and most all-sufficient seat and proper abode of all conceivable best attributes, and of all, which are many more, which cannot be conceived. I hold this as a matter of reason, though my imagination starts from it. I hold it firmly and absolutely, though it is the most difficult of all mysteries. I hold it from the actual experience of Thy blessings and mercies towards me, the evidences of Thy awful being and attributes, brought home continually to my reason, beyond the power of doubting or disputing. I hold it from that long and intimate familiarity with it, so that it is part of my rational nature to hold it; because I am so constituted and made up upon the idea of it, as a keystone, that not to hold it would be to break my mind to pieces. I hold it from that intimate perception of it in my conscience, as a fact present to me, that I feel it as easy to deny my own personality as the personality of God, and have lost my grounds for believing that I exist myself, if I deny existence to Him. I hold it because I could not bear to be without Thee, O my Lord and Life, because I look for blessings beyond thought by being with Thee. I hold it from the terror of being left in this wild world without stay or protection. I hold it from humble love to Thee, from delight in Thy glory and exaltation, from my desire that Thou shouldst be great and the only great one. I hold it for Thy sake, and because I love to think of Thee as so glorious, perfect, and beautiful. There is one God, and none other but He.

The Discipline of Meditation

Christ is gone away; He is not seen; we never saw Him, we only read and hear of Him. It is an old saying, 'Out of sight, out of mind'. Be sure, so it *will* be, so it *must* be with us, as regards our blessed Saviour, unless we make continual efforts all through the day to think of Him, His love, His precepts, His gifts, and His promises. We must recall to mind what we read in the Gospels and in holy books about Him; we must bring before us what we have heard in church; we must pray to God to enable us to do so, to bless the doing so, and to make us do so in a simple-minded, sincere, and reverential spirit. In a word, we must meditate, for all this is meditation; and this even the most unlearned person can do, and will do, if he has a will to do it.

Now of such meditation, or thinking over Christ's deeds and sufferings, I will say two things; the first of which would be too plain to mention, except that, did I not mention it, I might seem to forget it, whereas I grant it. It is this: that such meditation is not at all pleasant at first. I know it; people will find it at first very irksome, and their minds will gladly slip away to other subjects. True: but consider, if Christ thought your salvation worth the great sacrifice of voluntary sufferings for you, should not you think (what is your own concern) your own salvation worth the slight sacrifice of learning to meditate upon those sufferings? Can a less thing be asked of you, than, when He has done the work, that you should only have to believe in it and accept it?

And my second remark is this: that it is only by slow degrees that meditation is able to soften our hard hearts, and that the history of Christ's trials and sorrows really moves us. It is not once thinking of Christ or twice thinking of Christ that will do it. It is by going on quietly and steadily, with the thought of Him in our mind's eye, that by little and little we shall gain something of warmth, light, life and love. We shall not perceive ourselves changing. It will be like the unfolding of the leaves in spring. You do not see them grow; you cannot, by watching, detect it. But every day, as it passes, has done something for them; and you are able, perhaps, every morning to say that they are more advanced than yesterday. So it is with our souls; not indeed every morning, but at certain periods, we are able to see that we are more alive and religious than we were, though during the interval we were not conscious that we were advancing.

[43]

O Sacred Heart

O Sacred Heart of Jesus, I adore Thee in the oneness of the Personality of the Second Person of the Holy Trinity. Whatever belongs to the Person of Jesus, belongs therefore to God, and is to be worshipped with that one and the same worship which we pay to Jesus. He did not take on Him His human nature, as something distinct and separate from Himself, but as simply, absolutely, eternally His, so as to be included by us in the very thought of Him. I worship Thee, O Heart of Jesus, as being Jesus Himself, as being that Eternal Word in human nature which He took wholly and lives in wholly, and therefore in Thee. Thou art the Heart of the Most High made man. In worshipping Thee, I worship my Incarnate God, Emmanuel. I worship Thee, as bearing a part in that Passion which is my life, for Thou didst burst and break, through agony, in the Garden of Gethsemani, and Thy precious contents trickled out, through the veins and pores of the skin, upon the earth. And again, Thou hadst been drained all but dry upon the Cross; and then, after death, Thou wast pierced by the lance, and gavest out the small remains of that inestimable treasure, which is our redemption.

Absent yet Present

The thought of our Saviour absent yet present is like that of a friend taken from us, but, as it were in a dream, returned to us, though in this case not in dream but in reality and truth. When He was going away He said to His disciples, 'I will see you again, and your heart shall rejoice.' Yet He had at another time said, 'The days will come when the Bridegroom shall be taken from them, and then they shall fast in those days.' See what an apparent contradiction, such as attends the putting any high feeling into human language! They were to joy because Christ was come, and yet weep because He was away; that is, to have a feeling so refined, so strange and new, that nothing could be said of it, but that it combined in one all that was sweet and soothing in contrary human feelings, as commonly experienced. As some precious fruits of the earth are said to taste like all others at once, not as not being really distinct from all others, but as being thus best described, when we would come as near the truth as we can, so the state of mind which they are in who believe that the Son of God is here, yet away; is at the right hand of God, yet in His very flesh and blood among us; is present though invisible; is one of both joy and pain, or rather one far above either; a feeling of awe, wonder, and praise, which cannot be more suitably expressed than by the Scripture word *fear*; or by holy Job's words, though he spoke in grief, and not as being possessed of a blessing: 'Behold, I go forward, but He is not there; and backward, but I cannot perceive Him: on the left hand, where He doth work, but I cannot behold Him: He hideth Himself on the right hand, that I cannot see Him. Therefore am I troubled at His presence; when I consider, I am afraid of Him.'

I Adore Thee!

Thou didst know, in Thy eternal wisdom, that, in order to arrive at what was higher than any blessing which they were then enjoying, it was fitting, it was necessary, that they should sustain conflict and suffering. Thou knewest well, that unless Thou hadst departed, the Paraclete could not have come to them; and therefore Thou didst go, that they might gain more by Thy sorrowful absence than by Thy sensible visitations. I adore Thee, O Father, for sending the Son and the Holy Ghost! I adore Thee, O Son, and Thee, O Holy Ghost, for vouchsafing to be sent to us!

Discerning Christ's Presence

We must not only have faith in Him, but must wait on Him; not only must hope, but must watch for Him; not only love Him, but must long for Him; not only obey Him, but must look out, look up earnestly for our reward, which is Himself. We must not only make Him the Object of our faith, hope, and charity, but we must make it our duty not to believe the world, not to hope in the world, not to love the world . . .

They, then, watch and wait for their Lord, who are tender and sensitive in their devotion towards Him; who feed on the thought of Him, hang on His words; live in His smile, and thrive and grow under His hand. They are eager for His approval, quick in catching His meaning, jealous of His honour. They see Him in all things, expect Him in all events, and amid all the cares, the interests, and the pursuits of this life, still would feel an awful joy, not a disappointment, did they hear that He was on the point of coming . . .

You know there are subtle instincts in the inferior animals, by which they apprehend the presence of things which man cannot discern, as atmospheric changes or convulsions of the earth or their natural enemies, whom yet they do not actually see; and we consider the uneasiness or the terror which they exhibit to be a proof that there is something near them which is the object of the feeling, and is the evidence of its own reality. Well, in some such way the continuous watching and waiting for Christ, which Prophets, Apostles, and the Church built upon them, have manifested age after age, is a demonstration that the Object of it is not a dream or a fancy, but really exists; in other words, that He lives still, that He has ever lived, who was once upon earth, who died, who disappeared, who said He would come again.

In my Innermost Heart

O my God, Thou dost over-abound in mercy! To live by faith is my necessity, from my present state of being and from my sin; but Thou hast pronounced a blessing on it. Thou hast said that I am more blessed if I believe on Thee, than if I saw Thee. Give me to share that blessedness, give it to me in its fullness. Enable me to believe as if I saw; let me have Thee always before me as if Thou wert always bodily and sensibly present. Let me ever hold communion with Thee, my hidden, but my living God. Thou art in my innermost heart. Thou art the life of my life. Every breath I breathe, every thought of my mind, every good desire of my heart, is from the presence within me of the unseen God. By nature and by grace Thou art in me. I see Thee not in the material world except dimly, but I recognize Thy voice in my own intimate consciousness. I turn round and say Rabboni. O be ever thus with me; and if I am tempted to leave *Thee*, do not Thou, O my God, leave *me!*

Watching for Christ

I conceive it may be explained as follows: Do you know the feeling in matters of this life, of expecting a friend, expecting him to come and he delays? Do you know what it is to be in unpleasant company, and to wish for the time to pass away, and the hour strike when you may be at liberty? Do you know what it is to be in anxiety lest something should happen which may happen or may not, or to be in suspense about some important event, which makes your heart beat when you are reminded of it, and of which you think the first thing in the morning? Do you know what it is to have a friend in a distant country, to expect news of him, and to wonder from day to day what he is now doing, and whether he is well? Do you know what it is so to live upon a person who is present with you, that your eyes follow his, that you read his soul, that you see all its changes in his countenance, that you anticipate his wishes, that you smile in his smile, and are sad in his sadness, and are downcast when he is vexed, and rejoice in his successes? To watch for Christ is a feeling such as all these; as far as feelings of this world are fit to shadow out those of another.

He watches for Christ, who has a sensitive, eager, apprehensive mind; who is awake, alive, quick-sighted, zealous in seeking and honouring Him; who looks out for Him in all that happens, and who would not be surprised, who would not be over-agitated or over-whelmed, if he found that He was coming at once.

Consolation

'It is I: be not afraid.'

When I sink down in gloom or fear,
　Hope blighted or delay'd,
Thy whisper, Lord, my heart shall cheer,
　"Tis I; be not afraid!'

Or, startled at some sudden blow,
　If fretful thoughts I feel,
'Fear not, it is but I!' shall flow,
　As balm my wound to heal.

Nor will I quit Thy way, though foes
　Some onward pass defend;
From each rough voice the watchword goes,
　'Be not afraid! . . . a friend!'

And oh! when judgement's trumpet clear
　Awakes me from the grave,
Still in its echo may I hear,
　"Tis Christ; He comes to save.'

The Evocation of the Eternal

It is not a mere form of words, it is a great action, the greatest action that can be on earth. It is, not the invocation merely, but, if I dare use the word, the evocation of the Eternal. He becomes present on the altar in flesh and blood, before whom angels bow and devils tremble. This is that awful event which is the end, and is the interpretation, of every part of the solemnity. Words are necessary, but as means, not as ends; they are not mere addresses to the throne of grace, they are instruments of what is far higher, of consecration, of sacrifice. They hurry on, as if impatient to fulfil their mission. Quickly they go, the whole is quick; for they are all parts of one integral action. Quickly they go; for they are awful words of sacrifice, they are a work too great to delay upon; as when it was said in the beginning, 'What thou doest, do quickly.' Quickly they pass; for the Lord Jesus goes with them, as He passed along the lake in the days of his flesh, quickly calling first one and then another. Quickly they pass; because as the lightning which shineth from one part of the heaven unto the other, so is the coming of the Son of man. Quickly they pass; for they are the words of the Lord descending in the cloud, and proclaiming the Name of the Lord as He passes by, 'The Lord, the Lord God, merciful and gracious, long-suffering, and abundant in goodness and truth.' And as Moses on the mountain, so we too 'make haste and bow our heads to the earth, and worship.' So we, all around, each in his place, look out for the great Advent, 'waiting for the moving of the water.' Each in his place, with his own heart, with his own wants, with his own thoughts, with his own intention, with his own prayers, separate but concordant, watching what is going on, watching its progress, uniting in its consummation; not painfully and hopelessly following a hard form of prayer from beginning to end, but like a concert of musical instruments, each different, but concurring in a sweet harmony, we take our part with God's priest, supporting him, yet guided by him. There are little children there, and old men, and simple labourers, and students in seminaries, priests preparing for Mass; priests making their thanksgiving; there are innocent maidens, and there are penitents; but out of these many minds rises one eucharistic hymn, and the great Action is the measure and scope of it.

The Hidden Lord of Life

O my dear Saviour, would that I had any right to ask to be allowed to make reparation to Thee for all the unbelief of the world, and all the insults offered to Thy Name, Thy Word, Thy Church and the Sacrament of Thy Love! But, alas, I have a long score of unbelief and ingratitude of my own to atone for. Thou art in the Sacrifice of the Mass, Thou art in the Tabernacle, verily and indeed, in flesh and blood; and the world not only disbelieves, but mocks at this gracious truth. Thou didst warn us long ago by Thyself and by Thy Apostles that Thou wouldest hide Thyself from the world. The prophecy is fulfilled more than ever now; but *I* know what the world knows not. O accept my homage, my praise, my adoration! Let me at least not be found wanting. I cannot help the sins of others; but one at least of those whom Thou hast redeemed shall turn round and with a loud voice glorify God. The more men scoff, the more will I believe in Thee, the good God, the good Jesus, the hidden Lord of life, who hast done me nothing else but good from the very first moment that I began to live.

Fasting and Feasting

This too must be said concerning the connection of fasts and feasts in our religious service, viz. that that sobriety in feasting which previous fasting causes, is itself much to be prized, and especially worth securing. For in this does Christian mirth differ from worldly, that it is subdued; and how shall it be subdued except that the past keeps its hold upon us, and while it warns and sobers us, actually indisposes and tames our flesh against indulgence? In the world feasting comes first and fasting afterwards; men first glut themselves, and then loathe their excesses; they take their fill of good, and then suffer; they are rich that they may be poor; they laugh that they may weep; they rise that they may fall. But in the Church of God it is reversed; the poor *shall* be rich, the lowly shall be exalted, those that sow in tears shall reap in joy, those that mourn shall be comforted, those that suffer with Christ shall reign with Him; even as Christ (in our Church's words) 'went not up to joy, but first He suffered pain. He entered not into His glory before He was crucified. So truly our way to eternal joy is to suffer here with Christ, and our door to enter into eternal life is gladly to die with Christ, that we may rise again from death, and dwell with Him in everlasting life.' And what is true of the general course of our redemption is, I say, fulfilled also in the yearly and other commemorations of it. Our festivals are preceded by humiliation, that we may keep them duly; not boisterously or fanatically, but in a refined, subdued, chastised spirit, which is the true rejoicing in the Lord.

Loss and Gain

My God and Saviour, who wast thus deprived of the light of consolation, whose soul was dark, whose affections were left to thirst without the true object of them, and all this for man, take not from *me* the light of Thy countenance, lest I shrivel from the loss of it and perish in my infirmity. Who can sustain the loss of the Sun of the soul but Thou? Who can walk without light, or labour without the pure air, but Thy great Saints? As for me, alas, I shall turn to the creature for my comfort, if Thou wilt not give me Thyself. I shall not mourn, I shall not hunger or thirst after justice, but I shall look about for whatever is at hand, and feed on offal, or stay my appetite with husks, ashes, or chaff, which if they poison me not, at least nourish not. O my God, leave me not in that dry state in which I am; give me the comfort of Thy grace. How can I have any tenderness or sweetness, unless I have Thee to look upon?

The Sign of the Cross

Whene'er across this sinful flesh of mine
    I draw the Holy Sign,
All good thoughts stir within me, and renew
    Their slumbering strength divine;
Till there springs up a courage high and true
    To suffer and to do.

And who shall say, but hateful spirits around,
    For their brief hour unbound,
Shudder to see, and wail their overthrow?
    While on far heathen ground
Some lonely Saint hails the fresh odour, though
    Its source he cannot know.

Carry me Forward

O my God, let me never forget that seasons of consolation are refreshments here, and nothing more; not our abiding state. They will not remain with us, except in heaven. Here they are only intended to prepare us for doing and suffering. I pray Thee, O my God, to give them to me from time to time. Shed over me the sweetness of Thy Presence, lest I faint by the way; lest I find religious service wearisome, through my exceeding infirmity, and give over prayer and meditation; lest I go about my daily work in a dry spirit, or am tempted to take pleasure in it for its own sake, and not for Thee. Give me Thy Divine consolations from time to time; but let me not rest in them. Let me use them for the purpose for which Thou givest them. Let me not think it grievous, let me not be downcast, if they go. Let them carry me forward to the thought and the desire of heaven.

The Spiritual Vessel

To be *spiritual* is to live in the world of spirits – as St Paul says, 'Our conversation is in heaven'. To be *spiritually*-minded is to see by faith all those good and holy beings who actually surround us, though we see them not with our bodily eyes; to see them by faith as vividly as we see the things of earth – the green country, the blue sky, and the brilliant sunshine. Hence it is that, when saintly souls are favoured with heavenly visions, these visions are but the extraordinary continuations and the crown, by a divine intuition, of objects which, by the ordinary operation of grace, are ever before their minds.

These visions consoled and strengthened the Blessed Virgin in all her sorrows. The Angels who were around her understood her, and she understood them, with a directness which is not to be expected in their intercourse with us who have inherited from Adam the taint of sin. Doubtless; but still let us never forget that as she in her sorrows was comforted by Angels, so it is our privilege in the many trials of life to be comforted, in our degree, by the same heavenly messengers of the Most High; nay, by Almighty God Himself, the third Person of the Holy Trinity, who has taken on Himself the office of being our Paraclete, or Present Help.

Let all those who are in trouble take this comfort to themselves, if they are trying to lead a spiritual life. If they call on God, He will answer them. Though they have no earthly friend, they have Him, who, as He felt for His Mother when He was on the Cross, now that He is in His glory feels for the lowest and feeblest of His people.

Jesus the Hidden God

I adore Thee, O my God, who art so awful, because Thou art hidden and unseen! I adore Thee, and I desire to live by faith in what I do not see; and considering what I am, a disinherited outcast, I think it has indeed gone well with me that I am allowed, O my unseen Lord and Saviour, to worship Thee anyhow. O my God, I know that it is sin that has separated between Thee and me. I know it is sin that has brought on me the penalty of ignorance. Adam, before he fell, was visited by Angels. Thy Saints, too, who keep close to Thee, see visions, and in many ways are brought into sensible perception of Thy presence. But to a sinner such as I am, what is left but to possess Thee without seeing Thee? Ah, should I not rejoice at having that most extreme mercy and favour of possessing Thee at all? It is sin that has reduced me to live by faith, as I must at best, and should I not rejoice in such a life, O Lord my God? I see and know, O my good Jesus, that the only way in which I can possibly approach Thee in this world is the way of faith, faith in what Thou has told me, and I thankfully follow this only way which Thou hast given me.

In God's Hands

To Miss Hope-Scott

There is nothing like the blessedness of feeling oneself in God's hands, to do what He will with us – to be lodged there, without a will of our own, knowing that with Him we are safe.

You, and dear Papa, each of you has this greatest of mercies. Our Lord says, Peace I leave with you, My peace I give unto you. What can we ask for more?

Doubt not He will be with *you*, as He is with him.

Meanwhile, all your friends will go on praying.

———

God Knows

God knows what is my greatest happiness, but I do not. There is no rule about what is happy and good; what suits one would not suit another. And the ways by which perfection is reached vary very much; the medicines necessary for our souls are very different from each other. Thus God leads us by strange ways; we know He wills our happiness, but we neither know what our happiness is, nor the way. We are blind; left to ourselves we should take the wrong way; we must leave it to Him . . . O my God, I will put myself without reserve into Thy hands. Wealth or woe, joy or sorrow, friends or bereavement, honour or humiliation, good report or ill report, comfort or discomfort, Thy presence or the hiding of Thy countenance, all is good if it comes from Thee. Thou are Wisdom and Thou art love – what can I desire more?

True Worship

We know two things of the Angels – that they cry Holy, Holy, Holy, and that they do God's bidding. Worship and service make up their blessedness; and such is our blessedness in proportion as we approach them. But all exercises of mind which lead us to reflect upon and ascertain our state; to know what worship is, and why we worship; what service is, and why we serve; what our feelings imply, and what our words mean, tend to divert our minds from the one thing needful, unless we are practised and expert in using them. All proofs of religion, evidences, proofs of particular doctrines, scripture proofs, and the like – these certainly furnish scope for the exercise of great and admirable powers of mind, and it would be fanatical to disparage or disown them; but it requires a mind rooted and grounded in love not to be dissipated by them. As for truly religious minds, they, when so engaged, instead of mere disputing, are sure to turn inquiry into meditation, exhortation into worship, and argument into teaching.

The Occupation of Eternity

Eternal, Incomprehensible God, I believe, and confess, and adore Thee, as being infinitely more wonderful, resourceful, and immense, than this universe which I see. I look into the depths of space, in which the stars are scattered about, and I understand that I should be millions upon millions of years in creeping along from one end of it to the other, if a bridge were thrown across it. I consider the overpowering variety, richness, intricacy of Thy work; the elements, principles, laws, results which go to make it up. I try to recount the multitudes of kinds of knowledge, of sciences, and of arts of which it can be made the subject. And, I know, I should be ages upon ages in learning everything that is to be learned about this world, supposing me to have the power of learning it at all. And new sciences would come to light, at present unsuspected, as fast as I had mastered the old, and the conclusions of today would be nothing more than starting points of tomorrow. And I see moreover, and the more I examined it, the more I should understand, the marvellous beauty of these works of Thy hands. And so, I might begin again, after this material universe, and find a new world of knowledge, higher and more wonderful, in Thy intellectual creations, Thy angels and other spirits, and men. But all, all that is in these worlds, high and low, are but an atom compared with the grandeur, the height and depth, the glory, on which Thy saints are gazing in their contemplation of Thee. It is the occupation of eternity, ever new, inexhaustible, ineffably ecstatic, the stay and the blessedness of existence, thus to drink in and be dissolved in Thee.

Pray for me

Pray for me, O my friends; a visitant
  Is knocking his dire summons at my door,
The like of whom, to scare me and to daunt,
  Has never, never come to me before;
'Tis death – O loving friends, your prayers! – 'tis he! . . .
As though my very being had given way,
  As though I was no more a substance now,
And could fall back on nought to be my stay,
  (Help, loving Lord! Thou my sole Refuge, Thou),
And turn no whither, but must needs decay
  And drop from out the universal frame
Into that shapeless, scopeless, blank abyss.
  That utter nothingness, of which I came:
This is it that has come to pass in me:
  Oh, horror! this is it, my dearest, this;
So pray for me, my friends, who have not strength to pray.

Prayer for the Faithful Departed

O God of the Spirits of all flesh, O Jesu, Lover of souls, we recommend unto Thee the souls of all those Thy servants, who have departed with the sign of faith and sleep the sleep of peace. We beseech Thee, O Lord and Saviour, that, as in Thy mercy to them Thou becamest man, so now Thou wouldst hasten the time, and admit them to Thy presence above. Remember, O Lord, that they are Thy creatures, not made by strange gods, but by Thee, the only Living and True God; for there is no other God but Thou, and none that can equal Thy works. Let their souls rejoice in Thy light, and impute not to them their former iniquities, which they committed through the violence of passion, or the corrupt habits of their fallen nature. For, although they have sinned, yet they always firmly believed in the Father, Son, and Holy Ghost; and before they died, they reconciled themselves to Thee by true contrition and the Sacraments of Thy Church . . .

Come to their assistance, all ye Saints of God; gain for them deliverance from their place of punishment; meet them, all ye Angels; receive these holy souls, and present them before the Lord. Eternal rest give to them, O Lord. And may perpetual light shine on them.

May they rest in peace. Amen.

Jesus, May I Ever Love Thee

THE CONTEMPLATION OF CHRIST

True Kindness

The greatest acknowledgement we can make of the kindness of a superior, is to say that he acts as if he were personally interested in us. The mass of benevolent men are kind and generous, because it is their way to be so, irrespectively of the person whom they benefit. Natural temper, a flow of spirits, or a turn of good fortune, opens the heart, which pours itself out profusely on friend and enemy. They scatter benefits as they move along. Now, at first sight, it is difficult to see how our idea of Almighty God can be divested of these earthly notions, either that His goodness is imperfect, or that it is fated and necessary; and wonderful indeed, and adorable is the condescension by which He has met our infirmity. He has met and aided it in that same Dispensation by which He redeemed our souls. In order that we may understand that in spite of His mysterious perfections He has a separate knowledge and regard for individuals, He has taken upon Him the thoughts and feelings of our own nature, which we all understand *is* capable of such personal attachments. By becoming man, He has cut short the perplexities and the discussions of our reason on the subject, as if He would grant our objections for argument's sake, and supersede them by taking our own ground.

Love Incarnate

He, indeed, when man fell, might have remained in the glory which He had with the Father before the world was. But that unsearchable Love, which showed itself in our original creation, rested not content with a frustrated work, but brought Him down again from His Father's bosom to do His will, and repair the evil which sin had caused. And with a wonderful condescension He came, not as before in power, but in weakness, in the form of a servant, in the likeness of that fallen creature whom He purposed to restore. So He humbled Himself; suffering all the infirmities of our nature in the likeness of sinful flesh, all but a sinner – pure from all sin, yet subjected to all temptation – and at length becoming obedient unto death, even the death of the cross.

Born of a Woman

He came by a new and living way; not, indeed, formed out of the ground, as Adam was at the first, lest He should miss the participation of our nature, but selecting and purifying unto Himself a tabernacle out of that which existed. As in the beginning, woman was formed out of man by Almighty power, so now, by a like mystery, but a reverse order, the new Adam was fashioned from the woman. He was, as had been foretold, the immaculate 'seed of the woman', deriving His manhood from the substance of the Virgin Mary; as it is expressed in the articles of the Creed – 'conceived by the Holy Ghost, born of the Virgin Mary'.

Thus the Son of God became the Son of Man; mortal, but not a sinner; heir of our infirmities, not of our guiltiness; the offspring of the old race, yet 'the beginning of the' new 'creation of God'. Mary, His mother, was a sinner as others, and born of sinners; but she was set apart, 'as a garden inclosed, a spring shut up, a fountain sealed', to yield a created nature to Him who was her Creator. Thus He came into this world, not in the clouds of heaven, but born into it, born of a woman; He, the Son of Mary, and she (if it may be said), the mother of God.

The Hidden Years

What were the actual circumstances of His coming? His Mother is a poor woman; she comes to Bethlehem to be taxed, travelling, when her choice would have been to remain at home. She finds there is no room in the inn; she is obliged to betake herself to a stable; she brings forth her firstborn Son, and lays Him in a manger. That little babe, so born, so placed, is none other than the Creator of heaven and earth, the Eternal Son of God.

Well, He was born of a poor woman, laid in a manger, brought up to a lowly trade, that of a carpenter; and when He began to preach the Gospel, He had not a place to lay His head; lastly, He was put to death, to an infamous and odious death, the death which criminals then suffered.

For the three last years of His life, He preached, I say, the Gospel, as we read in Scripture; but He did not begin to do so till He was thrity years old. For the first thirty years of His life, He seems to have lived, just as a poor man would live now. Day after day, season after season, winter and summer, one year and then another, passed on as might happen to any of us. He passed from being a babe in arms to being a child, and then He became a boy, and so He grew up 'like a tender plant', increasing in wisdom and stature; and then He seems to have followed the trade of Joseph His reputed father; going on in an ordinary way without any great occurrence, till He was thirty years old. How very wonderful is all this! that He should live here, doing nothing great, so long; living here, as if for the sake of living; not preaching, or collecting disciples, or apparently in any way furthering the cause which brought Him down from heaven. Doubtless there were deep and wise reasons in God's counsels for His going on so long in obscurity; I only mean, that *we* do not know them.

The Hidden God

And it is remarkable that those who were about Him, seem to have treated Him as one of their equals. His brethren, that is, His near relations, His cousins, did not believe in Him. And it is very observable, too, that when He began to preach, and a multitude collected, we are told, 'When His friends heard of it, they went out to lay hold on Him; for they said, He is beside Himself.' They treated Him as we might be disposed, and rightly, to treat any ordinary person now, who began to preach in the streets. I say 'rightly', because such persons generally preach a *new* Gospel, and therefore must be wrong. Also, they preach without being sent, and against authority; all which is wrong too. Accordingly we are often tempted to say that such people are 'beside themselves', or mad, and not unjustly. It is often charitable to say so, for it is better to be mad than to be disobedient. Well, what we should say of such persons, this is what our Lord's friends said of Him. They had lived so long with Him, and yet did not know Him; did not understand what He was. They saw nothing to mark a difference between Him and them. He was dressed as others, He ate and drank as others, He came in and went out, and spoke, and walked, and slept, as others. He was in all respects a man, except that He did not sin; and this great difference the many would not detect, because none of us understands those who are much better than himself: so that Christ, the sinless Son of God, might be living close to us, and we not discover it.

I say that Christ, the sinless Son of God, might be living now in the world as our next door neighbour, and perhaps we not find it out. And this is a thought that should be dwelt on.

Our Highest Love

Christ has sanctioned and enjoined love and care for our relations and friends. Such love is a great duty; but should at any time His guidance lead us by a strange way, and the light of His providence pass on, and cast these objects of our earthly affection into the shade, then they must be at once in the shade to *us* – they must, for the time, disappear from our hearts. 'He that loveth father or mother more than Me, is not worthy of Me.' So He says; and at such times, though still loving them, we shall seem to hate them; for we shall put aside the thought of them, and act as if they did not exist. And in this sense an ancient and harsh proverb is true: we must always so love our friends as feeling that one day or other we may perchance be called upon to hate them – that is, forget them in the pursuit of higher duties . . .

If a person says it is painful thus to feel, and that it checks the spontaneous and continual flow of love towards our friends to have this memento sounding in our ears, we must boldly acknowledge that it *is* painful. It is a sad thought, not that we can ever be called upon actually to put away the love of them, but to have to act as if we did not love them – as Abraham when called on to slay his son. And this thought of the uncertainty of the future, doubtless, does tinge all our brightest affections (as far as this world is concerned) with a grave and melancholy hue. We need not shrink from this confession, remembering that this life is not our rest or happiness: '*that* remaineth' to come.

Christ Alone

He took other human friends, when He had given up His Mother – the twelve Apostles – as if He desired that in which He might sympathize. He chose them, as He says, to be 'not servants but friends'. He made them His confidants. He told them things which He did not tell others. It was His will to favour, nay, to indulge them, as a father behaves towards a favourite child. He made them more blessed than kings and prophets and wise men, from the things He told them. He called them 'His little ones', and preferred them for His gifts to the wise and prudent. He exulted, while He praised them, that they had continued with Him in His temptations, and as if in gratitude He announced that they should sit upon twelve thrones judging the twelve tribes of Israel. He rejoiced in their sympathy when His solemn trial was approaching. He assembled them about Him at the last supper, as if they were to support Him in it. 'With desire', He says, 'have I desired to eat this Pasch with you, before I suffer.' Thus there was an interchange of good offices, and an intimate sympathy between them. But it was His adorable will that they too should leave Him, that He should be left to Himself. One betrayed, another denied Him, the rest ran away from Him, and left Him in the hands of His enemies. Even after He had risen, none would believe in it. Thus He trod the winepress alone.

'To Whom shall we Go?'

After our Lord had declared what all who heard seemed to feel to be a hard doctrine, some in surprise and offence left Him. Our Lord said to the Twelve most tenderly, 'Will ye also go away?' St Peter promptly answered No: but observe on what ground He put it. He says, 'Lord to whom shall we go?' implying he must go somewhere. Christ had asked 'Will ye also go *away*?' He only asked about Peter's leaving *Himself*; but in Peter's thought to leave Him was to go somewhere else. He only thought of leaving Him by taking another god. That negative state of neither believing nor disbelieving, neither acting this way nor that, which is so much in esteem now, did not occur to his mind as possible. The fervent Apostle ignored the existence of scepticism. With him his course was at best but *a choice of difficulties* – of difficulties perhaps, but still a choice. He knew of no course without a choice – choice he must make. Somewhither he must go: whither else? If Christ could deceive him, to whom should he go? Christ's ways might be dark, His words often perplexing, but still he found in Him what He found nowhere else – amid difficulties a realization of his inward longings. 'Thou hast the words of eternal life.'

So far he saw. He might have misgivings at times; he might have permanent and in themselves insuperable objections; still in spite of such objections, in spite of the assaults of unbelief, on the whole, he saw that in Christ which was positive, real and satisfying. He saw it nowhere else. 'Thou', he says, 'hast the words of eternal life; and we *have believed* and *have* known that thou art the Christ, the Son of the Living God.' As if he said, 'We will stand by what we believed and knew yesterday – what we believed and knew the day before. A sudden gust of new doctrines, a sudden inroad of new perplexities, shall not unsettle us. We *have* believed, we *have* known: we cannot collect together all the evidence, but this is the abiding deep conviction of our minds. We feel that it is better, safer, truer, more pleasant, more blessed to cling to Thy feet, O merciful Saviour, than to leave Thee, Thou *canst not* deceive us: it is impossible. We will hope in Thee against hope, and believe in Thee against doubt, and obey Thee in spite of gloom.'

The Eternal Word

Our Saviour said all that need be said, but His Apostles understood Him not. Nay, when they made confession, and that in faith, and by the secret grace of God, and therefore acceptably to Christ, still they understood not fully what they said. St Peter acknowledged Him as the Christ, the Son of God. So did the centurion who was present at His crucifixion. Did that centurion, when He said, 'Truly, this was the Son of God', understand his own words? Surely not. Nor did St Peter, though he spoke, not through flesh and blood, but by the revelation of the Father. Had he understood, could he so soon after, when our Lord spoke of His passion which lay before Him, have presumed to 'take Him, and begin to rebuke Him'? Certainly he did not understand that our Lord, as being the Son of God, was not the creature of God, but the Eternal Word, the Only-begotten Son of the Father, one with Him in substance, distinct in Person.

Suffering with Christ

Jesus could bear His Cross alone, did He so will; but He permits Simon to help Him, in order to remind us that we must take part in His sufferings, and have a fellowship in His work. His merit is infinite, yet He condescends to let His people add their merit to it. The sanctity of the Blessed Virgin, the blood of the Martyrs, the prayers and penances of the Saints, the good deeds of all the faithful, take part in that work which, nevertheless, is perfect without them. He saves us by His blood, but it is through and with ourselves that He saves us. Dear Lord, teach us to suffer with Thee, make it pleasant to us to suffer for Thy sake, and sanctify all our sufferings by the merits of Thy own.

O Loving Wisdom

O loving wisdom of our God!
　When all was sin and shame,
A second Adam to the fight
　And to the rescue came.

O wisest love! that flesh and blood
　Which did in Adam fail,
Should strive afresh against the foe,
　Should strive and should prevail;

And that a higher gift than grace
　Should flesh and blood refine,
God's Presence and His very Self,
　And Essence all-divine.

O generous love! that He who smote
　In man for man the foe,
The double agony in man
　For man should undergo;

And in the garden secretly,
　And on the cross on high,
Should teach His brethren and inspire
　To suffer and to die.

The Atoning Sacrifice

The great and awful doctrine of the Cross of Christ, which we now commemorate, may fitly be called, in the language of figure, the *heart* of religion. The heart may be considered as the seat of life; it is the principle of motion, heat, and activity; from it the blood goes to and fro to the extreme parts of the body. It sustains the man in his powers and faculties; it enables the brain to think; and when it is touched, man dies. And in like manner the sacred doctrine of Christ's atoning Sacrifice is the vital principle on which the Christian lives, and without which Christianity is not. Without it no other doctrine is held profitably; to believe in Christ's divinity, or in His manhood, or in the Holy Trinity, or in a judgement to come, or in the resurrection of the dead, is an untrue belief, not Christian faith, unless we receive also the doctrine of Christ's sacrifice. On the other hand, to receive it presupposes the reception of other high truths of the Gospel besides; it involves the belief in Christ's true divinity, in His true incarnation, and in man's sinful state by nature; and it prepares the way to belief in the sacred eucharistic feast, in which He who was once crucified is ever given to our souls and bodies, verily and indeed, in His Body and in His Blood. But again, the heart is hidden from view; it is carefully and securely guarded; it is not like the eye set in the forehead, commanding all, and seen of all: and so in like manner the sacred doctrine of the atoning Sacrifice is not one to be talked of, but to be lived upon; not to be put forth irreverently, but to be adored secretly; not to be used as a necessary instrument in the conversion of the ungodly, or for the satisfaction of reasoners of this world, but to be unfolded to the docile and obedient; to young children, whom the world has not corrupted; to the sorrowful, who need comfort; to the sincere and earnest, who need a rule of life; to the innocent, who need warning; and to the established, who have earned the knowledge of it.

The Transfiguration

Light of the anxious heart,
    Jesus, Thou dost appear,
To bid the gloom of guilt depart,
    And shed Thy sweetness here.

Joyous is he, with whom,
    God's Word, Thou dost abide;
Sweet Light of our eternal home,
    To fleshly sense denied.

Brightness of God above!
    Unfathomable grace!
Thy Presence be a fount of love
    Within Thy chosen place.

To Thee, whom children see,
    The Father ever blest,
The Holy Spirit, One and Three,
    Be endless praise addrest.

The Power of the Cross

Because the Brazen Serpent in the wilderness healed by being looked at, men consider that Christ's Sacrifice saves by the mind's contemplating it. This is what they call casting themselves upon Christ – coming before Him simply and without self-trust, and being saved by faith. Surely we ought so to *come* to Christ; surely we must believe; surely we must look; but the question is, in what form and manner He *gives* Himself to us; and it will be found that, when He enters into us, glorious as He is Himself, pain and self-denial are His attendants. Gazing on the Brazen Serpent did not heal; but God's invisible communication of the gift of health to those who gazed. So also justification is wholly the work of God; it comes from God to us; it is a power exerted on our souls by Him, as the healing of the Israelites was a power exerted on their bodies. The gift must be brought *near* to us; it is not like the Brazen Serpent, a mere external, material, local sign; it is a spiritual gift, and, as being such, admits of being applied to us individually. Christ's Cross does not justify by being looked at, but by being applied; not by merely being beheld by faith, but by being actually set up within us, and that not by our act, but by God's invisible grace . . . The Cross must be brought home to us, not in word, but in power, and this is the work of the Spirit . . .

Reverence

I bow at Jesu's name, for 'tis the Sign
Of awful mercy towards a guilty line.
Of shameful ancestry, in birth defiled,
    And upwards from a child
Full of unlovely thoughts and rebel aims
    And scorn of judgement-flames,
How without fear can I behold my Life,
The Just assailing sin, and death-stain'd in the strife?

And so, albeit His woe is our release,
Thought of that woe aye dims our earthly peace;
The Life is hidden in a Fount of Blood!
    And this is tidings good
For souls, who, pierced that they have caused that woe,
    Are fain to share it too:
But for the many, clinging to their lot
Of worldly ease and sloth 'tis written 'Touch Me not.'

The Mystery of the Cross

To ———

I conceive that the Atonement is a 'mystery', a glorious 'mystery', to be gloried in *because* it is a mystery, to be received by a pure act of faith, inasmuch as reason does not *see how* the death of God Incarnate can stand instead of, can be a Vicarious Satisfaction for, the eternal death of his sinful brethren. And sad experience of the want of this faith in most men (for which ordinarily a deep sense of sin is required, which the multitude of sinners have not, not to speak of the need of an initial love of God) was what made St Paul give utterance to his glorying in the Cross, which was to the political Pharisee and Sadducee a stumbling block and to the proud, supercilious Greek foolishness. It was indeed the great proof and instance of God's love to man, but he gloried in it, not on this account, but because it was wisdom and love in a mystery, spoken against by the world, but the life of the believer.

'You, Corinthians', says St Paul 'must begin by humbling your intellect to a mystery, and your selfishness to mortification of soul and body, for in your pride and sensuality you have forgotten your pattern Christ crucified.' Now, with all that is good and spiritual in the Evangelical party, I think they have forgotten that the Cross of Christ is a 'mystery', and to be treated with deep reverence. Instead of this, they call it a 'manifestation' and flourish it about as a 'plan', a 'scheme', a great argument addressed to the world, and in itself exciting faith, the one instrument of God's grace, convincing, satisfying the reason, and thereby the means of conversion; whereas my great fear has been . . . lest this doctrine of a manifestation . . . should lead to a wish to destroy all mysteries . . . And I feel this strongly still.

Excuse me if I have said anything unfairly.

Make us to Trust

Jesus when He was nearest to His everlasting triumph, seemed to be farthest from triumphing. When He was nearest upon entering upon His Kingdom, and exercising all power in heaven and earth, He was lying dead in a cave of the rock . . . Make us to trust in Thee, O Jesus, that Thou wilt display in us a similar providence. Make us sure, O Lord, that the greater is our distress, the nearer we are to Thee. The more men scorn us, the more Thou dost honour us. The more men insult over us, the higher Thou wilt exalt us. The more they forget us, the more Thou dost keep us in mind. The more they abandon us, the closer Thou wilt bring us to Thyself.

The Good Shepherd

Our Lord found the sheep scattered; or, as He had said shortly before, 'All that ever came before Me are thieves and robbers'; and in consequence the sheep had no guide. Such were the priests and rulers of the Jews when Christ came; so that 'when He saw the multitudes He was moved with compassion on them because they fainted, and were scattered abroad as sheep having no shepherd' . . .

So was it all over the world when Christ came in His infinite mercy 'to gather in one the children of God that were scattered abroad'. And though for a moment, when in the conflict with the enemy the good Shepherd had to lay down His life for the sheep, they were left without a guide . . . yet He soon rose from death to live for ever, according to the prophecy which said, 'He that scattered Israel will gather him, as a shepherd doth his flock'. And as He says Himself in the parable before us, 'He calleth His own sheep by name and leadeth them out, and goeth before them, and the sheep follow Him, for they know His voice', so, on His resurrection, while Mary wept, He did call her by her name, and she turned herself and knew Him by the ear whom she had not known by the eye. So, too, He said, 'Simon, son of Jonas, lovest thou Me'? And He added, 'Follow Me'. And so again He and His Angel told the women, 'Behold He goeth before you into Galilee . . . go tell My brethren, that they go into Galilee, and there shall they see Me'.

From that time the good Shepherd, who took the place of the sheep, and died that they might live for ever, has gone before them: and 'they follow the Lamb whithersoever He goeth.

No earthly images can come up to the awful and gracious truth, that God became the Son of man – that the Word became flesh, and was born of a woman. This ineffable mystery surpasses human words. No titles of earth can Christ give to Himself, ever so lowly or mean, which will fitly show us His condescension. His act and deed is too great even for His own lips to utter it. Yet He delights in the image contained in the text, as conveying to us, in such degree as we can receive it, some notion of the degradation, hardship, and pain which He underwent for our sake.

True Witnesses

Christ's cause was the cause of light and religion, therefore His advocates and ministers were necessarily few. It is an old proverb (which even the heathen admitted) that 'the many are bad'. Christ did not confide His Gospel to the many; had He done so, we may even say, that it would have been at first sight a presumption against its coming from God. What was the chief work of His whole ministry, but that of choosing and separating *from* the multitude those who should be fit recipients of His Truth? As He went the round of the country again and again, through Galilee and Judea, He tried the spirits of men the while; and rejecting the baser sort who 'honoured Him with their lips while their hearts were far from Him', He specially chose twelve. The many He put aside for a while as an adulterous and sinful generation, intending to make one last experiment on the mass when the Spirit should come. But His twelve He brought near to Himself at once, and taught them. Then He sifted them, and one fell away; the eleven escaped as though by fire. *For* these eleven especially He rose again; He visited *them* and taught *them* for forty days; for in *them* He saw the fruit of the 'travail of His soul and was satisfied'; in them 'He saw His seed, He prolonged His days, and the pleasure of the Lord prospered in His hand.' These were His witnesses, for they had the love of the Truth in their hearts. 'I have chosen you', He says to them, 'and ordained you, that ye should go and bring forth fruit, and that your fruit should remain.'

So much then in answer to the question, Why did not Christ show Himself to the whole Jewish people after His resurrection? I ask in reply, What would have been the use of it? a mere passing triumph over sinners whose judgement is reserved for the next world. On the other hand, such a procedure would have interfered with, nay, defeated, the real object of His rising again, the propagation of His Gospel through the world by *means of His own intimate friends* and followers. And further, this preference of the few to the many seems to have been necessary from the nature of man, since all great works are effected, not by a multitude, but by the deep-seated resolution of a few; nay, necessary too from man's depravity, for, alas! popular favour is hardly to be expected for the cause of Truth.

[85]

Litany of the Resurrection (1)

Lord, have mercy.
Lord, have mercy.
Christ, have mercy.
Christ, have mercy.
Lord, have mercy.
Lord, have mercy.
Christ, hear us.
Christ, graciously hear us.

God the Father of Heaven,
Have mercy on us.
God the Son, Redeemer of the world,
Have mercy on us.
God the Holy Ghost,
Have mercy . . . [etc.]
Holy Trinity, one God,
Jesus, Redeemer of mankind,
Jesus, Conqueror of sin and Satan,
Jesus, triumphant over Death,
Jesus, the Holy and the Just,
Jesus, the Resurrection and the Life,
Jesus, the Giver of grace,
Jesus, the Judge of the world,
Who didst lay down Thy life for Thy sheep,
Who didst rise again the third day,
Who didst manifest Thyself to Thy chosen,
Visiting Thy blessed Mother,
Appearing to Magdalen while she wept,
Sending Thy angels to the holy women,
Comforting the Eleven,
Saying to them, Peace,
Breathing on them the Holy Ghost,
Confirming the faith of Thomas,
Committing Thy flock to Peter,
Speaking of the Kingdom of God . . .

Litany of the Resurrection (2)

. . . We sinners,
Beseech Thee, hear us.
That we may walk in newness of life,
We beseech Thee, hear us.
That we may advance in the knowledge of Thee,
We beseech . . . [etc.]
That we may grow in grace,
That we may ever have the bread of life,
That we may persevere unto the end,
That we may have confidence before Thee at Thy coming,
That we may behold Thy face with joy,
That we may be placed at Thy right hand in the judgement,
That we may have our lot with the saints,

Lamb of God, who takest away the sins of the world,
Spare us, O Lord.
Lamb of God, who takest away the sins of the world,
Graciously hear us, O Lord.
Lamb of God, who takest away the sins of the world,
Have mercy on us.
Christ, hear us.
Christ, graciously hear us.
Lord, have mercy.
Christ, have mercy.
Lord, have mercy.

Christ is risen, Alleluia.
He is risen indeed, and hath appeared unto Simon, Alleluia.

Let us pray

O God, who by Thy only-begotten Son hast overcome death, and
opened on us the way to eternal life, vouchsafe, we beseech Thee, so to
confirm us by Thy grace, that we may in all things walk after the
manner of those who have been redeemed from their sins, through the
same Jesus Christ our Lord. *Amen.*

Present in Spirit

'Touch me not,' He says to St Mary Magdalen, 'I am not yet ascended to my Father . . .' *Why* might not our Lord be touched *before* His ascension, and how *could* He be touched *after* it? But Christ speaks, it would seem, thus (if, as before, we might venture to paraphrase His sacred words) – 'Hitherto you have only known Me after the flesh. I have lived among you as a man. You have been permitted to approach Me sensibly, to kiss and embrace My feet, to pour ointment upon My head. But all this is at an end, now that I have died and risen again in the power of the Spirit. A glorified state of existence is begun in Me, and will soon be perfected. At present, though I bid you at one moment handle Me as possessed of flesh and bones, I vanish like a spirit at another; though I let one follower embrace My feet, and say, "Fear not", I repel another with the words, "Touch Me not." Touch Me not, for I am fast passing for your great benefit from earth to heaven, from flesh and blood into glory, from a natural body to a spiritual body. When I am ascended, then the change will be completed. To pass hence to the Father in My bodily presence, is to descend from the Father to you in spirit. When I am thus changed, when I am thus present to you, more really present than now, though invisibly, then you may touch Me – may touch Me, more really though invisibly, by faith, in reverence, through such outward approaches as I shall assign. Now you but see Me from time to time; when you see most of Me I am at best but "going in and out among you". Thou hast seen Me, Mary, but couldst not hold Me; thou hast approached Me, but only to embrace My feet, or to be touched by My hand; and thou sayest, "O that I knew where I might find Him, that I might come even to His seat! O that I might hold Him and not let Him go!" Henceforth this shall be; when I am ascended, thou shalt see nothing, thou shalt have everything. Thou shalt "sit down under My shadow with great delight, and My fruit shall be sweet to thy taste." Thou shalt have Me whole and entire. I will be near thee, I will be in thee; I will come into thy heart a whole Saviour, a whole Christ – in all My fullness as God and man – in the awful virtue of that Body and Blood, which has been taken into the Divine Person of the Word, and is indivisible from it.

Our Redeemer Liveth

What has been now said about the Ascension of our Lord, comes to this: that we are in a world of mystery, with one bright Light before us, sufficient for our proceeding forward through all difficulties. Take away this Light, and we are utterly wretched – we know not where we are, how we are sustained, what will become of us, and all that is dear to us, what we are to believe, and why we are in being. But with it we have all and abound. Not to mention the duty and wisdom of implicit faith in the love of Him who made and redeemed us, what is nobler, what is more elevating and transporting, than the generosity of heart which risks every thing on God's word, dares the powers of evil to their worst efforts, and repels the illusions of sense and the artifices of reason, by confidence in the truth of Him who has ascended to the right hand of the Majesty on high. What infinite mercy it is in Him, that He allows sinners such as we are, the privilege of acting the part of heroes rather than of penitents? Who are we 'that we should be able' and have opportunity 'to offer so willingly after this sort?' – 'Blessed', surely thrice blessed, 'are they who have not seen and yet have believed!' We will not wish for sight; we will enjoy our privilege; we will triumph in the leave given us to go forward, 'not knowing whither we go', knowing that 'this is the victory that overcometh the world, even our faith.' It is enough that our Redeemer liveth; that He has been on earth and will come again. On Him we venture our all; we can bear thankfully to put ourselves into His hands, our interests present and eternal, and the interests of all we love.

'He shall Glorify Me'

When our Lord was leaving His Apostles, and they were sorrowful, He consoled them by the promise of another Guide and Teacher, on whom they might rely instead of Him, and who should be more to them even than He had been. He promised them the Third Person in the Ever-blessed Trinity, the Holy Ghost, the Spirit of Himself and of His Father, who should come invisibly, and with the greater power and comfort, inasmuch as He was invisible; so that His presence would be more real and efficacious by how much it was more secret and inscrutable. At the same time this new and most gracious Comforter, while bringing a higher blessedness, would not in any degree obscure or hide what had gone before. Though He did more for the Apostles than Christ had done, He would not throw into the shade and supersede Him whom He succeeded. How could that be? who could come greater or holier than the Son of God? who could obscure the Lord of glory? how could the Holy Ghost, who was one with the Son, and the Spirit proceeding from the Son, do otherwise than manifest the Son, while manifesting Himself? how could He fail to illuminate the mercies and perfections of Him, whose death upon the Cross opened a way for Himself, the Holy Ghost, to be gracious to man also? Accordingly, though it was expedient that the Son should go away, in order that the Comforter might come, we did not lose the sight of the Son in the presence of the Comforter. On the contrary, Christ expressly announced to the Apostles concerning Him, in the words of the text, 'He shall glorify Me.'

Christ Hidden and Revealed

And when we look into our Saviour's conduct in the days of His flesh, we find that He purposely concealed that knowledge, which yet He gave; as if intending it should be enjoyed, but not at once; as if His words were to stand, but to wait awhile for their interpretation; as if reserving them for His coming, who at once was to bring Christ and His words into the light. Thus when the young ruler came to Him, and said, 'Good Master', He showed Himself more desirous of correcting him than of revealing Himself, desirous rather to make him weigh his words, than Himself to accept them. At another time, when He had so far disclosed Himself that the Jews accused Him of blasphemy, in that He, being a man, made Himself God, far from repeating and insisting on the sacred Truth which they rejected, He invalidated the terms in which He had conveyed it, intimating that even the prophets of the Old Testament were called gods as well as He. And when He stood before Pilate, He refused to bear witness to Himself, or say what He was, or whence He came.

Thus He was among them 'as he that serveth'. Apparently, it was not till after His resurrection, and especially after His ascension, when the Holy Ghost descended, that the Apostles understood who had been with them. When all was over they knew it, not at the time.

Now here we see, I think, the trace of a general principle, which comes before us again and again both in Scripture and in the world, that God's Presence is not discerned at the time when it is upon us, but afterwards, when we look back upon what is gone and over.

The Life was Manifested

The life of Christ brings together and concentrates truths concerning the chief good and the laws of our being, which wander idle and forlorn over the surface of the moral world, and often appear to diverge from each other. It collects the scattered rays of light, which, in the first days of creation, were poured over the whole face of nature, into certain intelligible centres, in the firmament of the heaven, to rule over the day and over the night, and to divide the light from the darkness. Our Saviour has in Scripture all those abstract titles of moral excellence bestowed upon Him which philosophers have invented. He is the Word, the Light, the Life, the Truth, Wisdom, the Divine Glory. St John announces 'The Life was manifested, and we *have seen* It.'

The New Beginning

Christ came . . . to gather together in one all the elements of good dispersed throughout the world, to make them His own, to illuminate them with Himself, to reform and refashion them into Himself. He came to make a new and better beginning of all things than Adam had been, and to be a fountain-head from which all good henceforth might flow. Hence it is said that 'in the dispensation of the fullness of times' Almighty God 'gathered together in one all things in Christ, both which are in heaven, and which are on earth.' How He became a new commencement to things in heaven, we know not; nor know we adequately in what way He recapitulated or ordered anew things on earth. But this we know, that, the world being under the dominion of Satan, and truth and goodness in it being but as gems in the mine, or rather as metal in the ore, He came to elicit, to disengage, to combine, to purify, to perfect. And, further than this, He came to new-create – to begin a new line, and construct a new kingdom on the earth: that what had as yet lain in sin, might become what it was at the first, and more than that . . . He took on Him our nature, that in God that nature might revive and be restored; that it might be new born, and, after being perfected on the Cross, might impart that which itself was, as an incorruptible seed, for the life of all who receive it in faith, till the end of time. Hence He is called in Scripture the Beginning of the Creation of God, the First-begotten of the dead, the First-fruits of the Resurrection.

Anima Christi

Soul of Christ, be my sanctification;
Body of Christ, be my salvation;
Blood of Christ, fill all my veins;
Water of Christ's side, wash out my stains;
Passion of Christ, my comfort be;
O good Jesu, listen to me;
In thy wounds I fain would hide,
Ne'er to be parted from Thy side;
Guard me, should the foe assail me;
Call me when my life shall fail me;
Bid me come to Thee above,
With Thy saints to sing Thy love,
  World without end. Amen.

When we See Him

'He hath no form nor comeliness, and when we see Him, there is no beauty that we should desire Him.' It is not His loss that we love Him not, it is our loss. He is All-blessed, whatever becomes of us. He is not less blessed because we are far from Him. It is we who are not blessed, except as we approach Him, except as we are like Him, except as we love Him. Woe unto us, if in the day in which He comes from heaven we see nothing desirable or gracious in His wounds; but instead, have made for ourselves an ideal blessedness, different from that which will be manifested to us in Him. Woe unto us, if we have made pride, or selfishness, or the carnal mind, our standard of perfection and truth; if our eyes have grown dim, and our hearts gross, as regards the true light of men, and the glory of the Eternal Father. May He Himself save us from our self-delusions, whatever they are, and enable us to give up this world, that we may gain the next – and to rejoice in Him, who had no home of His own, no place to lay His head, who was poor and lowly, and despised and rejected, and tormented and slain!

Jesus, May I Ever Love Thee

1. Place yourself in the presence of God, kneeling with your hands clasped.

2. Read slowly and devoutly Revelation 1.10–18.

3. Bring all you have read before you at once, as if you saw our Lord.

4. Then say, 'His head and hairs were white like white wool, and as snow.'

(1) Thy hair is white, O Jesus, because Thou art the Ancient of days, as the Prophet Daniel speaks. From everlasting to everlasting Thou art God. Thou didst come indeed to us as a little child – Thou didst hang upon the Cross at an age of life before as yet grey hairs come – but, O my dear Lord, there was always something mysterious about Thee, so that men were not quite sure of Thy age. The Pharisees talked of Thee as near fifty. For Thou hadst lived millions upon millions of years, and Thy face awfully showed it. And even when Thou wast a child, Thy hair shone so bright that people said, 'It is snow.'

(2) O my Lord, Thou art ever old, and ever young. Thou hast all perfection, and old age in Thee is ten thousand times more beautiful than the most beautiful youth. Thy white hair is an ornament, not a sign of decay. It is as dazzling as the sun, as white as the light, and as glorious as gold.

5. *Conclusion.* Jesus, may I ever love Thee, not with human eyes, but with the eyes of the Spirit, which sees not as man sees.

To Attempt is to Do

THE RISK OF DISCIPLESHIP

The Call of Christ (1)

All through our life Christ is calling us. He called us first in Baptism; but afterwards also; whether we obey His voice or not, He graciously calls us still. If we fall from our Baptism, He calls us to repent; if we are striving to fulfil our calling, He calls us on from grace to grace, and from holiness to holiness, while life is given us. Abraham was called from his home, Peter from his nets, Matthew from his office, Elisha from his farm, Nathanael from his retreat; we are all in course of calling, on and on, from one thing to another, having no resting-place, but mounting towards our eternal rest, and obeying one command only to have another put upon us. He calls us again and again, in order to justify us again and again – and again and again, and more and more, to sanctify and glorify us.

It were well if we understood this; but we are slow to master the great truth, that Christ is, as it were, walking among us, and by His hand, or eye, or voice, bidding us follow Him. We do not understand that His call is a thing which takes place now. We think it took place in the Apostles' days; but we do not believe in it, we do not look out for it in our own case. We have not eyes to see the Lord; far different from the beloved Apostle, who knew Christ even when the rest of the disciples knew Him not. When He stood on the shore after His resurrection, and bade them cast the net into the sea, 'that disciple whom Jesus loved saith unto Peter, It is the Lord.'

The Call of Christ (2)

Now what I mean is this: that they who are living religiously, have from time to time truths they did not know before, or had no need to consider, brought before them forcibly; truths which involve duties, which are in fact precepts, and claim obedience. In this and such like ways Christ calls us now. There is nothing miraculous or extraordinary in His dealings with us. He works through our natural faculties and circumstances of life. Still what happens to us in providence is in all essential respects what His voice was to those whom He addressed when on earth: whether He commands by a visible presence, or by a voice, or by our consciences, it matters not, so that we feel it to be a command. If it is a command, it may be obeyed or disobeyed; it may be accepted as Samuel or St Paul accepted it, or put aside after the manner of the young man who had great possessions.

And these Divine calls are commonly, from the nature of the case, sudden now, and as indefinite and obscure in their consequences as in former times. The accidents and events of life are, as is obvious, one special way in which the calls I speak of come to us; and they, as we all know, are in their very nature, and as the word accident implies, sudden and unexpected. A man is going on as usual; he comes home one day, and finds a letter, or a message, or a person, whereby a sudden trial comes on him, which, if met religiously, will be the means of advancing him to a higher state of religious excellence, which at present he as little comprehends as the unspeakable words heard by St Paul in paradise. By a trial we commonly mean, a something which, if encountered well, will confirm a man in his present way; but I am speaking of something more than this; of what will not only confirm him, but raise him into a high state of knowledge and holiness. Many persons will find it very striking, on looking back on their past lives, to observe what different notions they entertained at different periods, of what Divine truth was, what was the way of pleasing God, and what things were allowable or not, what excellence was, and what happiness. I do not scruple to say, that these differences may be as great as that which may be supposed to have existed between St Peter's state of mind when quietly fishing on the lake, or Elisha's when driving his oxen, and that new state of mind of each of them when called to be Apostle or Prophet.

To Attempt is To Do

There is a famous instance of a holy man of old time, who before his conversion felt indeed the excellence of purity, but could not get himself to say more in prayer than 'Give me chastity, but not yet.' I will not be inconsiderate enough to make light of the power of temptation of any kind, nor will I presume to say that Almighty God will certainly shield a man from temptation for his wishing it; but whenever men complain, as they often do, of the arduousness of a high virtue, at least it were well that they should first ask themselves the question, whether they desire to have it. We hear much in this day of the impossibility of heavenly purity – far be it from me to say that every one has not his proper gift from God, one after this manner, another after that – but, O ye men of the world, when ye talk, as ye do, so much of the impossibility of this or that supernatural grace, when you disbelieve in the existence of severe self-rule, when you scoff at holy resolutions, and affix a slur on those who make them, are you sure that the impossibility which you insist upon does not lie, not in nature, but in the will? Let us but will, and our nature is changed, 'according to the power that worketh in us'. Say not, in excuse for others or for yourselves, that you cannot be other than Adam made you; you have never brought yourselves to will it – you cannot bear to will it. You cannot bear to be other than you are. Life would seem a blank to you, were you other; yet what you are from not desiring a gift, this you make an excuse for not possessing it.

Let us take what trial we please – the world's ridicule or censure, loss of prospects, loss of admirers or friends, loss of ease, endurance of bodily pain – and recollect how easy our course had been, directly we had once made up our mind to submit to it; how simple all that remained became, how wonderfully difficulties were removed from without, and how the soul was strengthened inwardly to do what was to be done. But it is seldom we have heart to throw ourselves, if I may so speak, on the Divine Arm; we dare not trust ourselves on the waters, though Christ bids us. We have not St Peter's love to ask leave to come to Him upon the sea. When we once are filled with that heavenly charity, we can do all things, because we attempt all things – for to attempt is to do.

A Reflection on Failure

To Walter Mayers

Such a host of things has happened since I addressed you last, that I do not know how or where to begin . . . For some time, even when appearances were most favourable, I had a sort of foreboding what would happen. About two months before my trial, the probability of success in my own judgement declined to a first in mathematics and a second in classics; when I went up, to two seconds – after the examination to one second; the Class List came out, and my name was below the line.

. . . My failure was most remarkable. I will grant I was unwell, low-spirited, and very imperfect in my books; yet, when in the Schools, so great a depression came on me, that I could do nothing. I was nervous in the extreme, a thing I never before experienced, and did not expect – my memory was gone, my mind altogether confused. The Examiners behaved with great kindness to me, but nothing would do. I dragged a sickly examination from Saturday to Friday, and after all was obliged to retire from the contest.

I will not attempt to describe the peace of mind I felt when all was over. Before there was darkness and dread – I saw the cataract, to which I was hurrying without the possibility of a rescue. It was as if a surgical operation was day after day being carried on upon me, and tearing away something precious; and all the while '*omnes omnia bona dicebant, et laudabant fortunas meas*'. They looked at me, and envied me, and laughed at my fears, and could hardly believe them real.

There is a great difference between believing a thing to be good, and feeling it; now I am thankful to say, I am not only enabled to believe failure to be best for me, but God has given me to see and know it. I never could before get my mind to say heartily 'Give me neither poverty nor riches.' I think I can now say it from my soul. I think I see clearly that honour and fame are not desirable. God is leading me through life in the way best adapted for His glory and my own salvation. I trust I may have always the same content and indifference to the world, which is at present the *prevailing* principle in my heart – yet I have great fears of backsliding.

Success and Disappointment

Look through the Bible, and you will find God's servants, even though they began with success, end with disappointment; not that God's purposes or His instruments fail, but that the time for reaping what we have sown is hereafter, not here; that here there is no great visible fruit in any one man's lifetime. Moses, for instance, began with leading the Israelites out of Egypt in triumph; he ended at the age of an hundred and twenty years, before his journey was finished and Canaan gained, one among the offending multitudes who were overthrown in the wilderness. Samuel's reformations ended in the people's wilfully choosing a king like the nations around them. Elijah, after his successes, fled from Jezebel into the wilderness to mourn over his disappointments. Isaiah, after Hezekiah's religious reign, and the miraculous destruction of Sennacherib's army, fell upon the evil days of his son Manasseh. Even in the successes of the first Christian teachers, the Apostles, the same rule is observed. After all the great works God enabled them to accomplish, they confessed before their death that what they experienced, and what they saw before them, was reverse and calamity, and that the fruit of their labour would not be seen, till Christ came to open the books and collect His Saints from the four corners of the earth.

One Step at a Time

Act up to your light, though in the midst of difficulties, and you will be carried on, you do not know how far. Abraham obeyed the call and journeyed, not knowing whither he went; so we, if we follow the voice of God, shall be brought on step by step into a new world, of which before we had no idea. This is His gracious way with us: He gives, not all at once, but by measure and season, wisely. To him that hath, more shall be given. But we must begin at the beginning. Each truth has its own order; we cannot join the way of life at any point of the course we please; we cannot learn advanced truths before we have learned primary ones.

Growing towards Perfection

What is the peculiarity of our nature, in contrast with the inferior animals around us? It is that, though man cannot change what he is born with, he is a being of progress with relation to his perfection and characteristic good. Other beings are complete from their first existence, in that line of excellence which is allotted to them; but man begins with nothing realized (to use the word), and he has to make capital for himself by the exercise of those faculties which are his natural inheritance. Thus he gradually advances to the fullness of his original destiny. Nor is this progress mechanical, nor is it of necessity; it is committed to the personal efforts of each individual of the species; each of us has the prerogative of completing his inchoate and rudimental nature, and of developing his own perfection out of the living elements with which his mind began to be. It is his gift to be the creator of his own sufficiency; and to be emphatically self-made. This is the law of his being, which he cannot escape, and whatever is involved in that law he is bound, or rather he is carried on, to fulfil.

Moral Beauty

There is a physical beauty and a moral: there is a beauty of person, there is a beauty of our moral being, which is natural virtue; and in like manner there is a beauty, there is a perfection, of the intellect. There is an ideal perfection in these various subject matters, towards which individual instances are seen to rise, and which are the standards for all instances whatever. The Greek divinities and demigods, as the statuary has moulded them, with their symmetry of figure, and their high forehead and their regular features, are the perfection of physical beauty. The heroes, of whom history tells, Alexander, or Caesar, or Scipio, or Saladin, are the representatives of that magnanimity or self-mastery which is the greatness of human nature. Christianity too has its heroes, and in the supernatural order, and we call them Saints. The artist puts before him beauty of feature and form; the poet, beauty of mind; the preacher, the beauty of grace: then intellect too, I repeat, has its beauty, and it has those who aim at it . . .

This indeed is but a temporal object, and a transitory possession; but so are other things in themselves which we make much of and pursue. The moralist will tell us, that man, in all his functions, is but a flower which blooms and fades, except so far as a higher principle breathes upon him, and makes him and what he is, immortal. Body and mind are carried on into an eternal world by the gifts of Divine Munificence; but at first they do but fail in a failing world; and, if the powers of intellect decay, the powers of the body have decayed before them, and, if an Hospital or an Almshouse, though its end be secular, may be sanctified to the service of Religion, so surely may an University, were it nothing more than I have as yet described it. We attain to heaven by using this world well, though it is to pass away; we perfect our nature, not by undoing it, but by adding to it what is more than nature, and directing it towards aims higher than its own.

Inner Discipline

Our Saviour gives us a pattern which we are bound to follow. He was a far greater than John the Baptist, yet He came, not with St John's outward austerity – condemning the *display* of strictness or gloominess, that we, His followers, might fast the more in private, and be the more austere in our secret hearts. True it is, that such self-command, composure, and inward faith, are not learned in a day; but if they were, why should this life be given us? It is given us as a very preparation-time for obtaining them. Only look upon the world in this light – its sights of sorrows are to calm you, and its pleasant sights to try you. There is a bravery in thus going straightforward, shrinking from no duty little or great, passing from high to low, from pleasure to pain, and making your principles strong without their becoming formal. Learn to be as the Angel, who could descend among the miseries of Bethesda, without losing his heavenly purity or his perfect happiness. Gain healing from troubled waters. Make up your mind to the prospect of sustaining a certain measure of pain and trouble in your passage through life; by the blessing of God this will prepare you for it – it will make you thoughtful and resigned without interfering with your cheerfulness. It will connect you in your own thoughts with the Saints of Scripture, whose lot it was to be patterns of patient endurance; and this association brings to the mind a peculiar consolation.

The Purpose of Pain

The natural effect, then, of pain and fear, is to individualize us in our own minds, to fix our thoughts on ourselves, to make us selfish. It is through pain, chiefly, that we realize to ourselves, even our bodily organs; a frame entirely without painful sensations is (as it were) one whole without parts, and prefigures that future spiritual body which shall be the portion of the saints. And to this we most approximate in our youth, when we are not sensible that we are compacted of gross terrestrial matter, as advancing years convince us. The young reflect little upon themselves; they gaze around them, and live out of doors, and say they have souls, little understanding their words. 'They rejoice in their youth.' This, then, is the effect of suffering, that it arrests us: that it puts, as it were, a finger upon us to ascertain for us our own individuality. But it does no more than this; if such a warning does not lead us through the stirrings of our conscience heavenwards, it does but imprison us in ourselves and make us selfish.

Here, then, it is that the Gospel finds us; heirs to a visitation, which, sooner or later, comes upon us, turning our thoughts from outward objects, and so tempting us to idolize self, to the dishonour of that God whom we ought to worship, and the neglect of man whom we should love as ourselves. Thus it finds us, and it obviates this danger, not by removing pain, but by giving it new associations. Pain, which by nature leads us only to ourselves, carries on the Christian mind from the thought of self to the contemplation of Christ, His passion, His merits, and His pattern; and, thence, further to that united company of sufferers who follow Him and 'are what He is in this world'. He is the great Object of our faith; and, while we gaze upon Him, we learn to forget ourselves.

The Second Eve

It was fitting then in God's mercy that, as the woman began the *destruction* of the world, so woman should also begin its *recovery*, and that, as Eve opened the way for the fatal deed of the first Adam, so Mary should open the way for the great achievement of the second Adam, even our Lord Jesus Christ, who came to save the world by dying on the cross for it. Hence Mary is called by the holy Fathers a second and a better Eve, as having taken that first step in the salvation of mankind which Eve took in its ruin.

How, and when, did Mary take part, and the initial part, in the world's restoration? It was when the Angel Gabriel came to her to announce to her the great dignity which was to be her portion. St Paul bids us 'present our bodies to God as a reasonable service'. We must not only pray with our lips, and fast, and do outward penance, and be chaste in our bodies; but we must be obedient, and pure in our minds. And so, as regards the Blessed Virgin, it was God's will that she should undertake *willingly* and with *full understanding* to be the Mother of our Lord, and not to be a mere passive instrument whose maternity would have no merit and no reward. The higher our gifts, the heavier our duties. It was no light lot to be so intimately near to the Redeemer of men, as she experienced afterwards when she suffered with Him. Therefore, weighing well the Angel's words before giving her answer to them – first she asked whether so great an office would be a forfeiture of that Virginity which she had vowed. When the Angel told her no, then, with the full consent of a full heart, full of God's love to her and her own lowliness, she said, 'Behold the handmaid of the Lord, be it done unto me according to thy word.' It was by this consent that she became the *Gate of Heaven*.

Instruments of the Lord

In my present line of reading, then, I am doing what I can to remedy this defect in myself, and (if so be) in some others. And it is a very joyful thought which comes to me with a great force of confidence to believe that, in doing so, I am one out of the instruments which our gracious Lord is employing with a purpose of good towards us. I mean that I believe God has not (so I trust) abandoned this branch of His Church which He has set up in England, and that, though for our many sins He has brought us into captivity to an evil world, and sons of Belial are lords over us, yet from time to time He sends us judges and deliverers as in the days of Gideon and Barak. I do verily believe that some such movement is now going on, and that the Philistines are to be smitten, and, believing it, I rejoice to join myself to the army of rescue, as one of those who lapped with the tongue when the rest bowed down to drink. And in saying this I do not take anything to myself personally, because Scripture has many warnings to us that those need not be highest in God's future favour or fullest in grace who even are His chief instruments here. Solomon's history is quite proof enough that the builders of the Church are not necessarily His truest servants, though they are on the right side, but may be surpassed by those who seem to do little towards the work. And Barak's history gives us another lesson akin to it, which I think of general application – 'The Lord delivered Sisera into the hand of a woman' – and surely it is the prayers of those who have especial leisure for prayer which do the Church most service. Do not, my dear Aunt, let us lose the benefit of your continual prayers, as I am sure we do not, that God would be pleased for His dear Son's sake to make us useful to Him in our day, that we may not lose or abuse our opportunities or gifts, but may do the work which He means us to do, and that manfully; that we may have a single aim, a clear eye, and a strong arm, and a courageous heart, and may be blessed inwardly in our own souls, as well as prosper in the edification of the Church. I am quite sure it is by prayers such as yours, of those whom the world knows nothing of, that the Church is saved, and I know I have them in particular, as you have also mine, my dear Aunt, every morning and evening.

True Humility

Once more: that religion is in itself a weariness is seen even in the conduct of the better sort of persons, who really on the whole are under the influence of its spirit. So dull and uninviting is calm and practical religion, that religious persons are ever exposed to the temptation of looking out for excitements of one sort or other, to make it pleasurable to them. The spirit of the Gospel is a meek, humble, gentle, unobtrusive spirit. It doth not cry nor lift up its voice in the streets, unless called upon by duty so to do, and then it does it with pain. Display, pretension, conflict, are unpleasant to it. What then is to be thought of persons who are ever on the search after novelties to make religion interesting to them; who seem to find that Christian activity cannot be kept up without unchristian party-spirit, or Christian conversation without unchristian censoriousness? Why, this: that religion is to them as to others, taken by itself, a weariness, and requires something foreign to its own nature to make it palatable. Truly it is a weariness to the natural man to serve God humbly and in obscurity; it is very wearisome, and very monotonous, to go on day after day watching all we do and think, detecting our secret failings, denying ourselves, creating within us, under God's grace, those parts of the Christian character in which we are deficient; wearisome to learn modesty, love of insignificance, willingness to be thought little of, backwardness to clear ourselves when slandered, and readiness to confess when we are wrong; to learn to have no cares for this world, neither to hope nor to fear, but to be resigned and contented!

False Honour

Look into the history of the world, and what do you read there? Revolutions and changes without number, kingdoms rising and falling; and when without crime? States are established by God's ordinance, they have their existence in the necessity of man's nature; but when was one ever established, nay, or maintained, without war and bloodshed? Of all natural instincts, what is more powerful than that which forbids us to shed our fellows' blood? We shrink with natural horror from the thought of a murderer; yet not a government has ever been settled, or a state acknowledged by its neighbours, without war and the loss of life; nay, more than this, not content with unjustifiable bloodshed, the guilt of which must lie somewhere, instead of lamenting it as a grievous and humiliating evil, the world has chosen to honour the conqueror with its amplest share of admiration. To become a hero, in the eyes of the world, it is almost necessary to break the laws of God and man. Thus the deeds of the world are matched by the opinions and principles of the world: it adopts bad doctrine to defend bad practice; it loves darkness because its deeds are evil.

The Definition of a Gentleman

It is almost a definition of a gentleman to say he is one who never inflicts pain. This description is both refined and, as far as it goes, accurate. He is mainly occupied in merely removing the obstacles which hinder the free and unembarrassed action of those about him; and he concurs with their movements rather than takes the initiative himself. His benefits may be considered as parallel to what are called comforts or conveniences in arrangements of a personal nature: like an easy chair or a good fire, which do their part in dispelling cold and fatigue, though nature provides both means of rest and animal heat without them. The true gentleman in like manner carefully avoids whatever may cause a jar or a jolt in the minds of those with whom he is cast – all clashing of opinion, or collision of feeling, all restraint, or suspicion, or gloom, or resentment; his great concern being to make every one at their ease and at home. He has his eyes on all his company; he is tender towards the bashful, gentle towards the distant, and merciful towards the absurd; he can recollect to whom he is speaking; he guards against unseasonable allusions, or topics which may irritate; he is seldom prominent in conversation, and never wearisome. He makes light of favours while he does them, and seems to be receiving when he is conferring. He never speaks of himself except when compelled, never defends himself by a mere retort, he has no ears for slander or gossip, is scrupulous in imputing motives to those who interfere with him, and interprets everything for the best. He is never mean or little in his disputes, never takes unfair advantage, never mistakes personalities or sharp sayings for arguments, or insinuates evil which he dare not say out. From a long-sighted prudence, he observes the maxim of the ancient sage that we should ever conduct ourselves towards our enemy as if he were one day to be our friend. He has too much good sense to be affronted at insults, he is too well employed to remember injuries, and too indolent to bear malice. He is patient, forbearing, and resigned, on philosophical principles; he submits to pain, because it is inevitable, to bereavement, because it is irreparable, and to death, because it is his destiny.

The Practice of Love

It is obviously impossible to love all men in any strict and true sense. What is meant by loving all men, is to feel well-disposed to all men, to be ready to assist them, and to act towards those who come in our way, as if we loved them. We cannot love those about whom we know nothing; except indeed we view them in Christ, as the objects of His Atonement, that is, rather in faith than in love. And love, besides, is a habit, and cannot be obtained without actual *practice*, which on so large a scale is impossible. We see then how absurd it is when writers (as is the manner of some who slight the Gospel) talk magnificently about loving the whole human race with a comprehensive affection, of being the friends of all mankind, and the like. Such vaunting professions, what do they come to? that such men have certain benevolent *feelings* towards the world – feelings and nothing more – nothing more than unstable feelings, the mere offspring of an indulged imagination, which exist only when their minds are wrought upon, and are sure to fail them in the hour of need. This is not to love men, it is but to talk about love. The real love of man *must* depend on practice, and therefore, must begin by exercising itself on our friends around us, otherwise it will have no existence. By trying to love our relations and friends, by submitting to their wishes, though contrary to our own, by bearing with their infirmities, by overcoming their occasional way-wardness by kindness, by dwelling on their excellences, and trying to copy them, thus it is that we form in our hearts that root of charity, which, though small at first, may, like the mustard seed, at last even overshadow the earth.

The Love of This World

Many men indeed are open revilers of religion, or at least openly disobey its laws; but let us consider those who are of a more sober and conscientious cast of mind. They have a number of good qualities, and are in a certain sense and up to a certain point religious; but they do not watch. Their notion of religion is briefly this: loving God indeed, but loving this world too; not only doing their *duty*, but finding their chief and highest *good*, in that state of life to which it has pleased God to call them, resting in it, taking it as their portion. They serve God, and they seek Him; but they look on the present world as if it were the eternal, not a mere temporary, scene of their duties and privileges, and never contemplate the prospect of being separated from it. It is not that they forget God, or do not live by principle, or forget that the goods of this world are His gift; but they love them for their own sake more than for the sake of the Giver, and reckon on their remaining, as if they had that permanence which their duties and religious privileges have. They do not understand that they are called to be strangers and pilgrims upon the earth, and that their worldly lot and worldly goods are a sort of accident of their existence, and that they really have no property, though human law guarantees property to them. Accordingly, they set their heart upon their goods, be they great or little, not without a sense of religion the while, but still idolatrously. *This* is their fault – an identifying God with this world, and therefore an idolatry towards this world; and so they are rid of the trouble of looking out for their God, for they think they have found Him in the goods of this world. While, then, they are really praiseworthy in many parts of their conduct, benevolent, charitable, kind, neighbourly, and useful in their generation, nay, constant perhaps in the ordinary religious duties which custom has established, and while they display much right and amiable feeling, and much correctness in opinion, and are even in the way to improve in character and conduct as time goes on; . . . yet still it is plain that they love this world, would be loth to leave it, and wish to have more of its good things. They like wealth, and distinction, credit, and influence. They may improve in conduct, but not in aims; they advance, but they do not mount; they are moving on a low level, and were they to move on for centuries, would never rise above the atmosphere of this world.

[115]

The Meaning of Unworldliness

The world, then, is the enemy of our souls; first, because, however innocent its pleasures, and praiseworthy its pursuits may be, they are likely to engross us unless we are on our guard: and secondly, because in all its best pleasures, and noblest pursuits, the seeds of sin have been sown; an enemy hath done this; so that it is most difficult to enjoy the good without partaking of the evil also. As an orderly system of various ranks, with various pursuits and their several rewards, it is to be considered not sinful indeed, but dangerous to us. On the other hand, considered in reference to its principles and actual practices, it is really a sinful world. Accordingly, when we are bid in Scripture to shun the world, it is meant that we must be cautious, lest we love what is good in it too well, and lest we love the bad at all. However, there is a mistaken notion sometimes entertained, that the world is some particular set of persons, and that to shun the world is to shun them; as if we could point out, as it were, with the finger, what is the world, and thus could easily rid ourselves of one of our three great enemies. Men who are beset with this notion are often great lovers of the world notwithstanding, while they think themselves at a distance from it altogether. They love its pleasures, and they yield to its principles, yet they speak strongly against men of the world, and avoid them. They act the part of superstitious people, who are afraid of seeing evil spirits in what are considered haunted places, while these spirits are busy at their hearts instead, and they do not suspect it.

Not as the World Gives

The mind finds nothing to satisfy it in the employments and amusements of life, in its excitements, struggles, anxieties, efforts, aims, and victories. Supposing a man to make money, to get on in life, to rise in society, to gain power, whether in a higher or lower sphere, this does not suffice; he wants a home, he wants a centre on which to place his thoughts and affections, a secret dwelling-place which may soothe him after the troubles of the world, and which may be his hidden stay and support wherever he goes, and dwell in his heart, though it be not named upon his tongue. The world may seduce, may terrify, may mislead, may enslave, but it cannot really inspire confidence and love. There is no rest for us, except in quietness, confidence, and affection; and hence all men, without taking religion into account, seek to make themselves a home, as the only need of their nature, or are unhappy if they be without one. Thus they witness against the world, even though they be children of the world; witness against it equally with the holiest and most self-denying, who have by faith overcome it.

Here then Christ finds us, weary of that world in which we are obliged to live and act, whether as willing or unwilling slaves to it. He finds us needing and seeking a home, and making one, as we best may, by means of the creature, since it is all we can do. The world, in which our duties lie, is as waste as the wilderness, as restless and turbulent as the ocean, as inconstant as the wind and weather. It has no substance in it, but is like a shade or phantom; when you pursue it, when you try to grasp it, it escapes from you, or it is malicious and does you a mischief. We need something which the world cannot give: this is what we need, and this it is which the Gospel has supplied.

False Prosperity

Bad as it is to be languid and indifferent in our secular duties, and to account this religion, yet it is far worse to be the slaves of this world, and to have our hearts in the concerns of this world. I do not know anything more dreadful than a state of mind which is, perhaps, the characteristic of this country, and which the prosperity of this country so miserably fosters. I mean that ambitious spirit, to use a great word, but I know no other word to express my meaning – that low ambition which sets every one on the look-out to succeed and to rise in life, to amass money, to gain power, to depress his rivals, to triumph over his hitherto superiors, to affect a consequence and a gentility which he had not before, to affect to have an opinion on high subjects, to pretend to form a judgement upon sacred things, to choose his religion, to approve and condemn according to his taste, to become a partisan in extensive measures for the supposed temporal benefit of the community, to indulge the vision of great things which are to come, great improvements, great wonders: all things vast, all things new – this most fearfully earthly and grovelling spirit is likely, alas! to extend itself more and more among our countrymen – in intense, sleepless, restless, never-wearied, never-satisfied, pursuit of Mammon in one shape or other, to the exclusion of all deep, all holy, all calm, all reverent thoughts. *This* is the spirit in which, more or less (according to their different tempers), men do commonly engage in concerns of this world; and I repeat it, better, far better, were it to retire from the world altogether than thus to engage in it – better with Elijah to fly to the desert, than to serve Baal and Ashtoreth in Jerusalem.

The Danger of Riches (1)

The most obvious danger which worldly possessions present to our spiritual welfare is, that they become practically a substitute in our hearts for that One Object to which our supreme devotion is due. They are present; God is unseen. They are means at hand of effecting what we want: whether God will hear our petitions for those wants is uncertain; or rather I may say, certain in the negative. Thus they minister to the corrupt inclinations of our nature; they promise and are able to be gods to us, and such gods too as require no service, but, like dumb idiots, exalt the worshipper, impressing him with a notion of his own power and security. And in this consist their chief and most subtle mischief. Religious men are able to repress, nay extirpate sinful desires, the lust of the flesh and of the eyes, gluttony, drunkenness, and the like, love of amusements and frivolous pleasures and display, indulgence in luxuries of whatever kind; but as to wealth, they cannot easily rid themselves of a secret feeling that it gives them a footing to stand upon, an importance, a superiority; and in consequence they get attached to this world, lose sight of the duty of bearing the Cross, become dull and dim-sighted, and lose their delicacy and precision of touch, are numbed (so to say) in their fingers' ends, as regards religious interests and prospects. To risk all upon Christ's word seems somehow unnatural to them, extravagant, and evidences a morbid excitement; and death, instead of being a gracious, however awful release, is not a welcome subject of thought. They are content to remain as they are, and do not contemplate a change. They desire and mean to serve God, nay actually do serve Him in their measure; but not with the keen sensibilities, the noble enthusiasm, the grandeur and elevation of soul, the dutifulness and affectionateness towards Christ which become a Christian.

The Danger of Riches (2)

The danger of *possessing* riches is the carnal security to which they lead; that of *'desiring'* and *pursuing* them is, that an object of this world is thus set before us as the aim and end of life. It seems to be the will of Christ that His followers should have no aim or end, pursuit or business, merely of this world. Here, again, I speak as before, not in the way of precept, but of doctrine. I am looking at His holy religion as at a distance, and determining what is its general character and spirit, not what may happen to be the duty of this or that individual who has embraced it. It is His will that all we do should be done, not unto men, or to the world, or to self, but to His glory; and the more we are enabled to do this simply, the more favoured we are. Whenever we act with reference to an object of this world, even though it be ever so pure, we are exposed to the temptation – (not irresistible, God forbid!) still to the temptation – of setting our hearts upon obtaining it. And therefore, we call all such objects *excitements*, as stimulating us incongruously, casting us out of the serenity and stability of heavenly faith, attracting us aside by their proximity from our harmonious round of duties, and making our thoughts converge to something short of that which is infinitely high and eternal. Such excitements are of perpetual occurrence, and the mere undergoing them, so far from involving guilt in the act itself or its results, is the great business of life and the discipline of our hearts.

The Blessings of Poverty

But, in truth, that our Lord meant to speak of riches as being in some sense a calamity to the Christian, is plain . . . from His praises and recommendation on the other hand of poverty. For instance, 'Sell that ye have and give alms; provide yourselves bags which wax not old.' 'If thou wilt be perfect, go sell that thou hast and give to the poor, and thou shalt have treasure in heaven.' 'Blessed be ye poor: for yours is the kingdom of God.' 'When thou makest a dinner or a supper, call not thy friends, nor thy brethren, neither thy kinsmen, nor thy rich neighbours . . . but . . . call the poor, the maimed, the lame, the blind.' And in like manner, St James: 'Hath not God chosen the poor of this world rich in faith, and heirs of that kingdom which He hath promised to them that love Him?' Now, I cite these texts in the way of doctrine, not of precept. Whatever be the line of conduct they prescribe to this or that individual (with which I have nothing to do at present), so far seems clear, that according to the rule of the Gospel, the absence of wealth is, as such, a more blessed and a more Christian state than the possession of it.

_____

On Guard against Sin

A time of trial is often such a crisis in a man's spiritual history. It is a season when the iron is heated and malleable; one or two strokes serve to fashion it as a weapon for God or for Satan. Or in other words, if a man is then taken at unawares, an apparently small sin leads to consequences in years and ages to come so fearful, that one can hardly dare contemplate them. This may serve to make us understand the shortness and apparent simplicity of the trial which is sometimes represented in Scripture as sealing the fate of those who succumb to it; Saul's trial, for instance, or Esau's; as on the other hand, indefinitely great results may follow from one act of obedience, as Joseph's in resisting his master's wife, or David's in sparing the life of Saul. Such great occasions, good or evil, occur all through life, but especially in youth; and it were well if young persons would realize that they do occur and are momentous. Alas! what would they give afterwards, when they come to repent (not to speak of that most awful season, the future judgement, when they stand before God, and are shortly to enter heaven or hell), not to have done what in a moment of excitement they did – to recall the blasphemous avowal, or the guilty deed – to be what they then were and now are not, free to serve God, free from the brand and the yoke of Satan! How will they bitterly bewail that fascination, or delirium, or sophistry, which made them what they need not have been, had they used against it the arms which Christ gave them!

A Time to Repent

I fear a great number of persons who aim at retiring from the world's business, do so under the notion of their then enjoying themselves somewhat after the manner of the rich man in the Gospel, who said, 'Soul, thou hast much goods laid up for many years.' If this is the predominant aim of any one, of course I need not say that it is a fatal sin, for Christ Himself has said so. Others there are who are actuated by a mixed feeling: they are aware that they do not give so much time to religion as they ought; they do not live by rule; nay, they are not satisfied with the correctness or uprightness of some of the practices or customs which their way of life requires of them, and they get tired of active business as life goes on, and wish to be at ease. So they look to their last years as a time of retirement, in which they may *both* enjoy themselves *and* prepare for heaven. And thus they satisfy both their conscience and their love of the world. At present religion is irksome to them; but then, as they hope, duty and pleasure will go together. Now, putting aside all other mistakes which such a frame of mind evidences, let it be observed, that if they are at present *not* serving God with all their hearts, but look forward to a time when they shall do so, then it is plain that, when at length they *do* put aside worldly cares and turn to God, if ever they do, that time must necessarily be a time of deep humiliation, if it is to be acceptable to Him, not a comfortable retirement. Who ever heard of a pleasurable, easy, joyous repentance? It is a contradiction in terms. These men, if they do but reflect a moment, must confess that their present mode of life, supposing it be not so strict as it should be, is heaping up tears and groans for their last years, not enjoyment. The longer they live as they do at present, not only the more unlikely is it that they will repent at all; but even if they do, the more bitter, the more painful must their repentance be. The only way to escape suffering for sin hereafter is to suffer for it here. Sorrow here or misery hereafter; they cannot escape one or the other.

Living Sacrifices

Not for any worldly reason, then, not on any presumptuous or unbelieving motive, does the Christian desire leisure and retirement for his last years. Nay, he will be content to do without these blessings, and the highest Christian of all is he whose heart is so stayed on God, that he does not wish or need it; whose heart is so set on things above, that things below as little excite, agitate, unsettle, distress, and seduce him, as they stop the course of nature, as they stop the sun and moon, or change summer and winter. Such were the Apostles, who, as the heavenly bodies, went out 'to all lands', full of business, and yet full too of sweet harmony, even to the ends of the earth. Their calling was heavenly, but their work was earthly; they were in labour and trouble till the last; yet consider how calmly St Paul and St Peter write in their last days. St John, on the other hand, was allowed, in a great measure, to retire from the cares of his pastoral charge, and such, I say, will be the natural wish of every religious man, whether his ministry be spiritual or secular; but, not in order to *begin* to fix his mind on God, but merely because, though he may contemplate God as truly and be as holy in heart in active business as in quiet, still it is more becoming and suitable to meet the stroke of death (if it be allowed us) silently, collectedly, solemnly, than in a crowd and a tumult. And hence it is, among other reasons, that we pray in the Litany to be delivered ' from *sudden* death'.

On the whole, then, what I have said comes to this, that whereas Adam was sentenced to labour as a punishment, Christ has by His coming sanctified it as a means of grace and a sacrifice of thanksgiving, a sacrifice cheerfully to be offered up to the Father in His Name.

The Risk of Faith

Our duty as Christians lies in making ventures for eternal life without the absolute certainty of success . . . This, indeed, is the very meaning of the word 'venture'; for that is a strange venture which has nothing in it of fear, risk, danger, anxiety, uncertainty. Yes, so it certainly is; and in this consists the excellence and nobleness of *faith*; this is the very reason why *faith* is singled out from other graces, and honoured as the especial means of our justification, because its presence implies that we have the heart to make a venture.

If, then, faith be the essence of a Christian life, and if it be what I have now described, it follows that our duty lies in risking upon Christ's word what we have for what we have not; and doing so in a noble, generous way, not indeed rashly or lightly, still without knowing accurately what we are doing, not knowing either what we give up, nor again what we shall gain; uncertain about our reward, uncertain about our extent of sacrifice, in all respects leaning, waiting upon Him, trusting in Him to fulfil His promise, trusting in Him to enable us to fulfil our own vows, and so in all respects proceeding without carefulness or anxiety about the future.

The Sting of Conscience

To Mrs J. Mozley

I have gone through a great deal of pain, and have been very much cut up. The one predominant distress upon me has been this unsettlement of mind I am causing. This is a thing that has haunted me day by day. And for days I had a literal pain in and about my heart, which I suppose at any moment I could bring on again. I have been overworked lately. The translation of St Athanasius is, I am glad to say, just coming to an end, and I shall (so be it) relax. I suppose I need it. This has been a very trying year.

. . . Besides the pain of unsettling people, of course I feel the loss I am undergoing in the good opinion of my friends and well-wishers, though I can't tell how much I feel this. It is the shock, surprise, terror, forlornness, disgust, scepticism to which I am giving rise; the differences of opinion, division of families – all this it is that makes my heart ache.

. . . I cannot make out that I have any motive but a sense of indefinite risk to my soul in remaining where I am. A clear conviction of the substantial identity of Christianity and the Roman system has now been on my mind for a full three years. It is more than five years since the conviction first came on me, though I struggled against it and overcame it. I believe all my feelings and wishes are against change. I have nothing to draw me elsewhere. I hardly ever was at a Roman service; even abroad I knew no Roman Catholics. I have no sympathies with them as a party. I am giving up everything. I am not conscious of any resentment, disgust, or the like, to repel me from my present position; and I have no dreams whatever – far from it indeed. I seem to be throwing myself away.

Great Acts Take Time

I felt altogether the force of the maxim of St Ambrose, *'Non in dialecticâ complacuit Deo salvum facere populum suum'*; – I had a great dislike of paper logic. For myself, it was not logic that carried me on; as well might one say that the quicksilver in the barometer changes the weather. It is the concrete being that reasons; pass a number of years, and I find my mind in a new place; how? the whole man moves; paper logic is but the record of it. All the logic in the world would not have made me move faster towards Rome than I did; as well might you say that I have arrived at the end of my journey, because I see the village church before me, as venture to assert that the miles, over which my soul had to pass before it got to Rome, could be annihilated, even though I had had some far clearer view than I then had, that Rome was my ultimate destination. Great acts take time. At least this is what I felt in my own case . . .

Recalling God's Presence

Years that are past bear in retrospect so much of fragrance with them, though at the time perhaps we saw little in them to take pleasure in; or rather we did not, could not realize that we *were* receiving pleasure, though we received it. We received pleasure, because we were in the presence of God, but we knew it not; we knew not what we received; we did not bring home to ourselves or reflect upon the pleasure we were receiving; but afterwards, when enjoyment is past, reflection comes in. We feel at the time; we recognize and reason afterwards. Such, I say, is the sweetness and softness with which days long passed away fall upon the memory, and strike us. The most ordinary years, when we seemed to be living for nothing, these shine forth to us in their very regularity and orderly course. What was sameness at the time, is now stability; what was dullness, is now a soothing calm; what seemed unprofitable, has now its treasure in itself; what was but monotony, is now harmony; all is pleasing and comfortable, and we regard it all with affection. Nay, even sorrowful times (which at first sight is wonderful) are thus softened and illuminated afterwards: yet why should they not be so, since then, more than at other times, our Lord is present, when He seems leaving His own to desolateness and orphanhood?

Lead, Kindly Light

THE MEANING OF HOLINESS

———

Who can Save Me?

O my Lord, I sink down almost in despair, in utter remorse certainly and disgust at myself, that I so utterly neglect these means which Thou hast put into my hands, content to let things take their course, as if grace would infallibly lead to glory without my own trouble in the matter. What shall I say to Thee, O my Saviour! except that I am in the chains of habit, feeble, helpless, stunted, growthless, and as if I were meant to walk through life, as the inferior creatures, with my face down to the earth, on hands and feet, or crawling on, instead of having an erect posture and a heavenward face? O give me what I need – contrition for all those infinitely numerous venial sins, negligences, slovenliness, which are the surest foreboding that I am not of Thy predestinate. Who can save me from myself but Thou?

Inner Cleanliness

You say well that you are unclean. But in what time do you propose to become otherwise? Do you expect in this life ever to be clean? Yes, in one sense, by the presence of the Holy Ghost within you; but that presence we trust you have now. But if by 'clean', you mean free from that infection of nature, the least drop of which is sufficient to dishonour all your services, clean you never will be till you have paid the debt of sin, and lose that body which Adam has begotten. Be sure that the longer you live, and holier you become, you will only perceive that misery more clearly. The less of it you have, the more it will oppress you; its full draught does but confuse and stupefy you; as you come to yourself, your misery begins. The more your soul becomes one with Him who deigns to dwell within it, the more it sees with His eyes . . . To the end of the longest life you are still a beginner. What Christ asks of you is not sinlessness, but diligence. Had you lived ten times your present age, ten times more service would be required of you. Every day you live longer, more will be required. If He were to come today, you would be judged up to today. Did He come tomorrow, you would be judged up to tomorrow. Were the time put off a year, you would have a year more to answer for. You cannot elude your destiny, you cannot get rid of your talent; you are to answer for your opportunities, whatever they may be, not more nor less. You cannot be profitable to Him even with the longest life; you can show faith and love in an hour.

True Holiness

God alone can claim the attribute of holiness. Hence we say in the Hymn, 'Tu solus sanctus', 'Thou only art holy'. By holiness we mean the absence of whatever sullies, dims, and degrades a rational nature; all that is most opposite and contrary to sin and guilt.

We say that God alone is *holy*, though in truth *all* His high attributes are possessed by Him in that fullness, that it may be truly said that He alone has them. Thus, as to goodness, our Lord said to the young man, 'None is good but God alone.' He too alone is Power, He alone is Wisdom, He alone is Providence, Love, Mercy, Justice, Truth. This is true; but holiness is singled out as His special prerogative, because it marks more than His other attributes, not only His superiority over all His creatures, but emphatically His separation from them. Hence we read in the Book of Job, 'Can man be justified compared with God, or he that is born of a woman appear clean? Behold, even the moon doth not shine, and the stars are not pure, in His sight.' 'Behold, among His saints none is unchangeable, and the heavens are not pure in His sight.'

This we must receive and understand in the first place; but secondly we know too that, in His mercy, He has communicated in various measures His great attributes to His rational creatures, and, first of all, as being most necessary, holiness. Thus Adam, from the time of his creation, was gifted, over and above his nature as man, with the grace of God, to unite him to God, and to make him holy. Grace is therefore called holy grace; and, as being holy, it is the connecting principle between God and man. Adam in Paradise might have had knowledge, and skill, and many virtues; but these gifts did not unite him to his Creator. It was holiness that united him, for it is said by St Paul, 'Without holiness no man shall see God.'

Whom the Lord Loves

'He opened His mouth and said, Blessed are the poor in spirit, for theirs is the kingdom of heaven. Blessed are they that mourn, for they shall be comforted. Blessed are the meek . . . Blessed are they which do hunger and thirst after righteousness . . . Blessed are the merciful . . . Blessed are the pure in heart . . . Blessed are the peacemakers.' And lastly, 'Blessed are ye when men shall revile you and persecute you, and shall say all manner of evil against you falsely for My sake. Rejoice, and be exceeding glad; for great is your reward in heaven; for so persecuted they the prophets which were before you.' And by contrast, He added, 'But woe unto you that are rich, for ye have received your consolation. Woe unto you that are full, for ye shall hunger. Woe unto you that laugh now, for ye shall mourn and weep. Woe unto you when all men shall speak well of you, for so did their fathers unto the false prophets.'

At another time He spoke thus: 'Sell that ye have, and give alms.' 'If thou wilt be perfect, go and sell that thou hast, and give to the poor.' 'It is easier for a camel to go through the eye of a needle, than for a rich man to enter into the kingdom of God.' 'Whosoever will be chief among you, let him be your servant.' 'If any man will come after Me, let him deny himself, and take up his cross, and follow Me.' And, in a word, the doctrine of the Gospel, and the principle of it, is thus briefly stated by the Apostle in the words of the Wise Man: 'Whom the Lord loveth He chasteneth, and scourgeth every son whom He receiveth. If ye endure chastening, God dealeth with you as with sons . . . If ye be without chastisement, *whereof all are partakers*, then are ye bastards, and not sons.' Can words speak it plainer, that, as certainly as temporal prosperity is the gift of the Law, so also are hardship and distress the gift of the Gospel?

Take up thy portion, then, Christian soul, and weigh it well, and learn to love it. Thou wilt find, if thou art Christ's, in spite of what the world fancies, that after all, even at this day, endurance, in a special sense, *is* the lot of those who offer themselves to be servants of the King of sorrows.

The Brand of Cain

I bear upon my brow the sign
   Of sorrow and of pain;
Alas! no hopeful cross is mine,
   It is the brand of Cain.

The course of passion, and the fret
   Of godless hope and fear –
Toil, care, and guilt – their hues have set,
   And fix'd their sternness there.

Saviour! wash out the imprinted shame;
   That I no more may pine,
Sin's martyr, though not meet to claim
   Thy cross, a saint of Thine.

Endurance

There is an inward world into which they enter who come near to Christ, though to men in general they seem the same as before. They hold the same place as before in the world's society; their employments are the same, their ways, their comings-in and goings-out. If they were high in rank, they are still high; if they were in active life, they are still active; if they were wealthy, they still have wealth. They have still great friends, powerful connections, ample resources, fair name in the world's eye; but if they have drunk of Christ's cup, and tasted the bread of His Table in sincerity, it is not with them as in time past. A change has come over them, unknown indeed to themselves, except in its effects, but they have a portion in destinies to which other men are strangers, and, as having destinies, they have conflicts also. They drank what looked like a draught of this world, but it associated them in hopes and fears, trials and purposes, above this world. They came as for a blessing, and they have found a work. They are soldiers in Christ's army; they fight against 'things that are seen', and they have 'all these things against them'. To their surprise, as time goes on, they find that their lot is changed. They find that in one shape or other adversity happens to them. If they refuse to afflict themselves, God afflicts them. One blow falls, they are startled; it passes over, it is well; they expect nothing more. Another comes; they wonder; 'Why is this?' they ask; they think that the first should be their security against the second; they bear it, however; and it passes too. Then a third comes; they almost murmur; they have not yet mastered the great doctrine that endurance is their portion. O simple soul, is it not the law of thy being to endure since thou camest to Christ? Why camest thou but to endure? Why didst thou taste His heavenly feast, but that it might work in thee? Why didst thou kneel beneath His hand, but that He might leave on thee the print of His wounds? Why wonder then that one sorrow does not buy off the next? Does one drop of rain absorb the second? Does the storm cease because it has begun? Understand thy place in God's kingdom, and rejoice, not complain, that in thy day thou hast thy lot with Prophets and Apostles.

Self-surrender

We cannot change ourselves; this we know full well, or, at least, a very little experience will teach us. God alone can change us; God alone can give us the desires, affections, principles, views, and tastes which a change implies: this, too, we know . . . What then is it that we who profess religion lack? I repeat it, this: a willingness to *be* changed, a willingness to suffer (if I may use such a word), to suffer Almighty God to change us . . . But when a man comes to God to be saved, then, I say, the essence of true conversion is a *surrender* of himself, an unreserved, unconditional surrender; and this is a saying which most men who come to God cannot receive. They wish to be saved, but in their own way; they wish (as it were) to capitulate upon terms, to carry off their goods with them; whereas the true spirit of faith leads a man to look off from self to God, to think nothing of his own wishes, his present habits, his importance or dignity, his rights, his opinions, but to say, 'I put myself into Thy hands, O Lord; make Thou me what Thou wilt; I forget myself; I divorce myself from myself; I am dead to myself; I will follow Thee.' . . . Here is the very voice of self-surrender, 'What wilt thou have me to do? Take Thy own way with me; whatever it be, pleasant or painful, I will do it.'

Law and Grace

There are two opposite errors: one, the holding that salvation is not of God; the other, that it is not in ourselves. Now it is remarkable that the maintainers of both the one and the other error, whatever their differences in other respects, agree in this – in depriving a Christian life of its mysteriousness. He who believes that he can please God of himself, or that obedience can be performed by his own powers, of course has nothing more of awe, reverence, and wonder in his personal religion than when he moves his limbs and uses his reason, though he might well feel awe then also. And in like manner he also who considers that Christ's passion once undergone on the Cross absolutely secured his own personal salvation, may see mystery indeed in that Cross (as he ought), but he will see no mystery, and feel little solemnity, in prayer, in ordinances, or in his attempts at obedience. He will be free, familiar, and presuming, in God's presence. Neither will 'work out their salvation with fear and trembling'; for neither will realize, though they use the words, that God is in them 'to will and to do'. Both the one and the other will be content with a low standard of duty: the one, because he does not believe that God requires much; the other, because he thinks that Christ in His own person has done all. Neither will honour and make much of God's Law: the one, because he brings down the Law to his own power of obeying it; the other, because he thinks that Christ has taken away the Law by obeying it in his stead. They only feel awe and true seriousness who think that the Law remains; that it claims to be fulfilled by them; and that it can be fulfilled in them through the power of God's grace. Not that any man alive arises up to that perfect fulfilment, but that such fulfilment is not impossible; that it is begun in all true Christians; that they are all tending to it; are growing into it; and are pleasing to God because they are becoming, and in proportion as they are becoming like Him who, when He came on earth in our flesh, fulfilled the Law perfectly.

———

I Must Change

I know, O my God, I must change, if I am to see Thy face! I must undergo the change of death. Body and soul must die to this world. My real self, my soul, must change by a true regeneration. None but the holy can see Thee. Like Peter, I cannot have a blessing now, which I shall have afterwards. 'Thou canst not follow me now, but thou shalt follow hereafter.' Oh, support me, as I proceed in this great, awful, happy change, with the grace of Thy unchangeableness. My unchangeableness here below is perseverance in changing. Let me day by day be moulded upon Thee, and be changed from glory to glory, by ever looking towards Thee, and ever leaning on Thy arm. I know, O Lord, I must go through trial, temptation, and much conflict, if I am to come to Thee. I know not what lies before me, but I know as much as this. I know, too, that if Thou art not with me, my change will be for the worse, not for the better. Whatever fortune I have, be I rich or poor, healthy or sick, with friends or without, all will turn to evil if I am not sustained by the Unchangeable; all will turn to good if I have Jesus with me, yesterday and today the same, and for ever.

Inner Conversion

When I was fifteen (in the autumn of 1816) a great change of thought took place in me. I fell under the influences of a definite creed, and received into my intellect impressions of dogma, which, through God's mercy, have never been effaced or obscured. Above and beyond the conversations and sermons of the excellent man, long dead, who was the human means of this beginning of divine faith in me, was the effect of the books which he put into my hands, all of the school of Calvin. One of the first books I read was a work of Romaine's; I neither recollect the title nor the contents, except one doctrine, which of course I do not include among those which I believe to have come from a divine source, viz. the doctrine of final perseverance. I received it at once, and believed that the inward conversion of which I was conscious (and of which I still am more certain than that I have hands and feet) would last into the next life, and that I was elected to eternal glory. I have no consciousness that this belief had any tendency whatever to lead me to be careless about pleasing God. I retained it till the age of twenty-one, when it gradually faded away; but I believe that it had some influence on my opinions, in the direction of those childish imaginations which I have already mentioned, viz. in isolating me from the objects which surrounded me, in confirming me in my mistrust of the reality of material phenomena, and making me rest in the thought of two and two only supreme and luminously self-evident beings, myself and my Creator; for while I considered myself pre-destined to salvation, I thought others simply passed over, not predestined to eternal death. I only thought of the mercy to myself.

Open to God

A true Christian may almost be defined as one who has a ruling sense of God's presence within him. As none but justified persons have that privilege, so none but the justified have that practical perception of it. A true Christian, or one who is in a state of acceptance with God, is he who, in such sense, has faith in Him, as to live in the thought that He is present with him – present not externally, not in nature merely, or in providence, but in his innermost heart, or in his *conscience*. A man is justified whose conscience is illuminated by God, so that he habitually realizes that all his thoughts, all the first springs of his moral life, all his motives, and his wishes, are open to Almighty God. Not as if he was not aware that there is very much in him impure and corrupt, but he wishes that all that is in him should be bare to God. He believes that it is so, and he even joys to think that it is so, in spite of his fear and shame at its being so. He alone admits Christ into the shrine of his heart; whereas others wish, in some way or other, to be by themselves, to have a home, a chamber, a tribunal, a throne, a self where God is not – a home within them which is not a temple, a chamber which is not a confessional, a tribunal without a judge, a throne without a king – that self may be king and judge; and that the Creator may rather be dealt with and approached as though a second party, instead of His being that true and better self, of which self itself should be but an instrument and minister.

In a New Light

O what a new world of thought she had entered! It occupied her mind from its very novelty. Everything looked dull and dim by the side of it; her brother had ever been dinning into her ears that maxim of the heathen, 'Enjoy the present, trust nothing to the future.' She indeed could not enjoy the present with that relish which he wished, and she had not any trust in the future either; but this volume spoke a different doctrine. There she learned the very opposite to what Aristo taught, viz. that the present must be sacrificed for the future; that what is seen must give way to what is believed. Nay, more, she drank in the teaching which at first seemed so paradoxical, that even present happiness and present greatness lie in relinquishing what at first sight seems to promise them; that the way to true pleasure is, not through self-indulgence, but through mortification; that the way to power is weakness, the way to success failure, the way to wisdom foolishness, the way to glory dishonour. She saw that there was a higher beauty than that which the order and harmony of the natural world revealed, and a deeper peace and calm than that which the exercise, whether of the intellect or of the purest human affection, can supply . . . Life and death, action and suffering, fortunes and abilities, all had now a new meaning and application. As the skies speak differently to the philosopher and the peasant, as a book of poems to the imaginative and to the cold and narrow intellect, so now she saw her being, her history, her present condition, her future, in a new light, which no one else could share with her. But the ruling sovereign thought of the whole was He, who exemplified all this wonderful philosophy in Himself.

Prayer for the Light of Truth

O my God, I confess that *Thou canst* enlighten my darkness. I confess that Thou *alone* canst. I *wish* my darkness to be enlightened. I do not know whether Thou wilt: but that Thou canst and that I wish, are sufficient reasons for me to *ask*, what Thou at least hast not forbidden my asking. I hereby promise that by Thy grace which I am asking, I will embrace whatever I at length feel certain is the truth, if ever I come to be certain. And by Thy grace I will guard against all self-deceit which may lead me to take what nature would have, rather than what reason approves.

True Happiness

The Christian's *lot* is one of sorrow, but as the regenerate *life* with him is happiness, so is the gift of natural life also. We live, therefore we are happy; *upon* this life of ours come joys and sorrows; and in proportion as we are favourites of God, it is sorrow that comes, not joy. Still after all considered in ourselves, that we live; that God breathes in us; that we exist in Him; that we think and act; that we have the means of life; that we have food, and sleep, and raiment, and lodging; and that we are not lonely, but in God's Church, and are sure of brethren by the very token of our having a Father which is in heaven; so far, rejoicing is the very condition of our being, and all pain is little more than external, not reaching to our inmost heart. So far all men almost are on a level, seasons of sickness excepted. Even delicate health and feebleness of life does not preclude these pleasures. And as to seasons of sickness, or even long and habitual pain or disease, the good Lord can compensate for them in His own way by extraordinary supplies of grace, as in early times He made even the torments of Christians in persecution literally pleasant to them. He who so ordered it, that even the red-hot iron did feel pleasant to the martyrs after a while, cannot fail of means to support His servants when life becomes a burden. But, generally speaking, it is a happiness, and that to all ranks. High and low, rich and poor, have the same refreshment in their pilgrimage. Hunger is as pleasantly appeased by the low as by the high, on coarse fare as on delicate. Sleep is equally the comfort and recruiting of rich and poor. We eat, drink, and sleep whether we are in sorrow or in joy, in anxiety or in hope. Our natural life is the type of our spiritual life, and thus, in a literal as well as higher sense, we may bless Him 'who saveth our life from destruction, and crowneth us with mercy and loving kindness; who satisfieth our mouth with good things, making us young and lusty as an eagle.'

God is With Us

To Mrs J. Mozley

Why should I distress your kind heart with all my miseries? Yet you must know them, to avoid the greater misery of looking at me externally, and wondering and grieving over what seems incomprehensible. Shall I add that, distressing as is my state, it has not once come upon me to say, O that I had never begun to read theology! O that I had never meddled in ecclesiastical matters! O that I had never written the Tracts, etc! I lay no stress on this, but state it . . . Of course the human heart is mysterious. I may have some deep evil in me which I cannot fathom; I may have done some irreparable thing which demands punishment; but may not one humbly trust that the earnest prayers of many good people will be heard for me? May not one resign oneself to the event, whatever it turns out to be? May one not hope and believe, though one does not see it, that God's hand is in the deed, if a deed there is to be; that He has a purpose, and will bring it to good, and will show us that it is good, in His own time? Let us not doubt, may we never have cause to doubt, that He is with us. Continually do I pray that He would discover to me if I am under a delusion: what can I do more? What hope have I but in Him? To whom should I go? Who can do me any good? Who can speak a word of comfort but He? Who is there but looks on me with a sorrowful face? but He can lift up the light of His countenance upon me. All is against me – may He not add Himself as an adversary! May He tell me, may I listen to Him, if His will is other than I think it to be!

That Mysterious Presence

That mysterious Presence of God which encompasses us, which is in us, and around us, which is in our heart, which enfolds us as though with a robe of light, hiding our scarred and discoloured souls from the sight of Divine Purity, and making them shining as the Angels; and which flows in upon us too by means of all forms of beauty and grace which this visible world contains, in a starry host or (if I may so say) a milky way of divine companions, the inhabitants of Mount Zion where we dwell.

Lead, Kindly Light

Lead, kindly Light, amid the encircling gloom
   Lead Thou me on!
The night is dark, and I am far from home –
   Lead Thou me on!
Keep Thou my feet; I do not ask to see
The distant scene – one step enough for me.

I was not ever thus, nor pray'd that Thou
   Shouldst lead me on.
I loved to choose and see my path, but now
   Lead Thou me on!
I loved the garish day, and, spite of fears,
Pride ruled my will: remember not past years.

So long Thy power hath blest me, sure it still
   Will lead me on,
O'er moor and fen, o'er crag and torrent, till
   The night is gone;
And with the morn those angel faces smile
Which I have loved long since, and lost awhile.

True Religion

True religion is a hidden life in the heart; and though it cannot exist without deeds, yet these are for the most part secret deeds, secret charities, secret prayers, secret self-denials, secret struggles, secret victories. Of course in proportion as persons are brought out into public life, they will be seen and scrutinized, and (in a certain sense) known more; but I am talking of the ordinary condition of people in private life, such as our Saviour was for thirty years; and these look very like each other. And there are so many of them, that unless we get very near them, we cannot see any distinction between one and another; we have no means to do so, and it is no business of ours. And yet, though we have no right to judge others, but must leave this to God, it is very certain that a really holy man, a true saint, though he looks like other men, still has a sort of secret power in him to attract others to him who are like-minded, and to influence all who have any thing in them like him. And thus it often becomes a test, whether we are like-minded with the Saints of God, whether they have influence over us. And though we have seldom means of knowing at the time who are God's own Saints, yet after all is over we have; and then on looking back on what is past, perhaps after they are dead and gone, if we knew them, we may ask ourselves what power they had over us, whether they attracted us, influenced us, humbled us, whether they made our hearts burn within us. Alas! too often we shall find that we were close to them for a long time, had means of knowing them, and knew them not; and that is a heavy condemnation on us, indeed.

Hidden Sainthood

Andrew is scarcely known except by name; while Peter has ever held the place of honour all over the Church; yet Andrew brought Peter to Christ. And are not the Blessed Angels unknown to the world? and is not God Himself, the Author of all good, hid from mankind at large, partially manifested and poorly glorified, in a few scattered servants here and there? and His Spirit, do we know whence It cometh, and whither It goeth? and though He has taught men whatever there has been of wisdom among them from the beginning, yet when He came on earth in visible form, even then it was said of Him, 'The world knew Him not'. His marvellous providence works beneath a veil, which speaks but an untrue language; and, to see Him who is the Truth and the Life, we must stoop underneath it, and so in our turn hide ourselves from the world. They who present themselves at kings' courts, pass on to the inner chambers, where the gaze of the rude multitude cannot pierce; and we, if we would see the King of kings in His glory, must be content to disappear from the things that are seen. Hid are the saints of God; if they are known to men, it is accidentally, in their temporal offices, as holding some high earthly station, or effecting some mere civil work, not as saints. St Peter has a place in history, far more as a chief instrument of a strange revolution in human affairs, than in his true character, as a self-denying follower of his Lord, to whom truths were revealed which flesh and blood could not discern.

True Perfection

It is the saying of holy men that, if we wish to be perfect, we have nothing more to do than to perform the ordinary duties of the day well. A short road to perfection – short, not because easy, but because pertinent and intelligible. There are no short ways to perfection, but there are sure ones.

I think this is an instruction which may be of great practical use to persons like ourselves. It is easy to have vague ideas what perfection is, which serve well enough to talk about, when we do not intend to aim at it; but as soon as a person really desires and sets about seeking it himself, he is dissatisfied with anything but what is tangible and clear, and constitutes some sort of direction towards the practice of it.

We must bear in mind what is meant by perfection. It does not mean any extraordinary service, anything out of the way, or especially heroic – not all have the opportunity of heroic acts, of sufferings – but it means what the word perfection ordinarily means. By perfect we mean that which has no flaw in it, that which is complete, that which is consistent, that which is sound – we mean the opposite to imperfect. As we know well what *im*perfection in religious service means, we know by the contrast what is meant by perfection.

True Greatness

Do you desire to be great? make yourselves little. There is a mysterious connection between real advancement and self-abasement. If you minister to the humble and despised, if you feed the hungry, tend the sick, succour the distressed; if you bear with the froward, submit to insult, endure ingratitude, render good for evil, you are, as by a divine charm, getting power over the world and rising among the creatures. God has established this law. Thus He does His wonderful works. His instruments are poor and despised; the world hardly knows their names, or not at all. They are busied about what the world thinks petty actions, and no one minds them.

Grace has Done its Part

Moses, the patriot fierce, became
   The meekest man on earth,
To show us how love's quick'ning flame
   Can give our souls new birth.

Moses, the man of meekest heart,
   Lost Canaan by self-will,
To show, where Grace has done its part,
   How sin defiles us still.

Thou, who hast taught me in Thy fear,
   Yet seest me frail at best,
O grant me loss with Moses here,
   To gain his future rest!

An Innocent Faith

Observe the lesson which we gain for ourselves from the history of the Blessed Virgin; that the highest graces of the soul may be matured in private, and without those fierce trials to which the many are exposed in order to their sanctification. So hard are our hearts, that affliction, pain, and anxiety are sent to humble us, and dispose us towards a true faith in the heavenly word, when preached to us. Yet, it is only our extreme obstinacy of unbelief which renders this chastisement necessary. The aids which God gives under the Gospel Covenant, have power to renew and purify our hearts, without uncommon providences to discipline us into receiving them. God gives His Holy Spirit to us silently; and the silent duties of every day (it may be humbly hoped) are blest to the sufficient sanctification of thousands, whom the world knows not of. The Blessed Virgin is a memorial of this; and it is consoling as well as instructive to know it. When we quench the grace of Baptism, then it is that we need severe trials to restore us. This is the case of the multitude, whose best estate is that of chastisement, repentance, supplication, and absolution, again and again. But, there are those, who go on in a calm and unswerving course, learning day by day to love Him who has redeemed them, and overcoming the sin of their nature by his heavenly grace, as the various temptations to evil successively present themselves. And, of these undefiled followers of the Lamb, the Blessed Mary is the chief. Strong in the Lord, and in the power of his might, she 'staggered not at the promise of God through unbelief'; she believed when Zacharias doubted – with a faith like Abraham's she believed and was blessed for her belief, and had the performance of those things which were told her by the Lord. And when sorrow came upon her afterwards, it was but the blessed participation of her Son's sacred sorrows, not the sorrow of those who suffer for their sins.

If we, through God's unspeakable gift, have in any measure followed Mary's innocence in our youth, so far let us bless Him who enabled us.

True Blessedness

Today we celebrate the Annunciation of the Virgin Mary; when the Angel Gabriel was sent to tell her that she was to be the Mother of our Lord . . . Then it was that Mary gave utterance to her feelings in the Hymn which we read in the Evening Service. How many and complicated must they have been! In her was now to be fulfilled that promise which the world had been looking out for during thousands of years. The Seed of the woman, announced to guilty Eve, after long delay, was at length appearing upon earth, and was to be born of her. In her the destinies of the world were to be reversed, and the serpent's head bruised. On her was bestowed the greatest honour ever put upon any individual of our fallen race. God was taking upon Him her flesh, and humbling Himself, to be called Her offspring – such is the deep mystery! She of course would feel her own inexpressible unworthiness; and again, her humble lot, her ignorance, her weakness in the eyes of the world. And she had moreover, we may well suppose, that purity and innocence of heart, that bright vision of faith, that confiding trust in her God, which raised all these feelings to an intensity which we, ordinary mortals, cannot understand.

We cannot understand them; we repeat her hymn day after day – yet consider for an instant in how different a mode *we* say it from that in which she at first uttered it. *We* even hurry it over, and do not think of the meaning of those words which came from the most highly favoured, awfully gifted of the children of men.

'My soul doth magnify the Lord, and my spirit hath rejoiced in God my Saviour. For he hath regarded the low estate of His hand-maiden: for behold, from henceforth all generations shall call me blessed. For He that is mighty hath done to me great things; and holy is His name. And His mercy is on them that fear Him from generation to generation.'

The Sanctity of Marriage

But there is another portion of the original punishment of woman, which may be considered as repealed when Christ came. It was said to the woman, 'Thy husband shall rule over thee'; a sentence which has been strikingly fulfilled. Man has strength to conquer the thorns and thistles which the earth is cursed with, but the same strength has ever proved the fulfilment of the punishment awarded to the woman. Look abroad through the Heathen world, and see how the weaker half of mankind has every where been tyrannized over and debased by the strong arm of force. Consider all those eastern nations, which have never at any time reverenced it, but have heartlessly made it the slave of every bad and cruel purpose. Thus the serpent has triumphed, making the man still degrade himself by her who originally tempted him, and her, who then tempted, now suffer from him who was seduced. Nay, even under the light of revelation, the punishment on the woman was not removed at once. Still (in the words of the curse), her husband ruled over her. The very practice of polygamy and divorce, which was suffered under the patriarchal and Jewish dispensations, proves it.

But when Christ came as the seed of the woman, He vindicated the rights and honour of His Mother . . . the slavery is done away with. St Peter bids the husband 'give honour unto the wife, *because* the weaker, in that both are heirs of the grace of life.'

Accordingly, from that time, Marriage has not only been restored to its original dignity, but even gifted with a spiritual privilege, as the outward symbol of the heavenly union subsisting betwixt Christ and His Church.

Moderation

Another part of the character under review is, what our translation calls moderation: 'Let your moderation be known unto all men', or, as it may be more exactly rendered, your consideration, fairness, or equitableness. St Paul makes it a part of a Christian character to have a reputation for candour, dispassionateness, tenderness towards others. The truth is, as soon and in proportion as a person believes that Christ is coming, and recognizes his own position as a stranger on earth, who has but hired a lodging in it for a season, he will feel indifferent to the course of human affairs. He will be able to look on, instead of taking a part in them. They will be nothing to him. He will be able to criticize them, and pass judgement on them, without partiality. This is what is meant by 'our moderation' being acknowledged by all men. Those who have strong interests one way or the other, cannot be dispassionate observers and candid judges. They are partisans; they defend one set of people, and attack another. They are prejudiced against those who differ from them, or who thwart them. They cannot make allowances, or show sympathy for them. But the Christian has no keen expectations, no acute mortifications. He is fair, equitable, considerate towards all men, because he has no temptation to be otherwise. He has no violence, no animosity, no bigotry, no party feeling. He knows that his Lord and Saviour must triumph; he knows that He will one day come from heaven, no one can say how soon. Knowing then the end to which all things tend, he cares less for the road which is to lead to it. When we read a book of fiction we are much excited with the course of the narrative till we know how things will turn out; but when we do the interest ceases. So is it with the Christian. He knows Christ's battle will last till the end; that Christ's cause will triumph in the end; that His Church will last till He comes. He knows what is truth and what is error, where is safety and where is danger; and all this clear knowledge enables him to make concessions, to own difficulties, to do justice to the erring . . . He does not fear; fear it is that makes men bigots, tyrants, and zealots; but for the Christian, it is his privilege, as he is beyond hopes and fears, suspense and jealousy, so also to be patient, cool, discriminating, and impartial; so much so, that this very fairness marks his character in the eyes of the world, is 'known unto all men'.

Brighten our Declining Day

O God, unchangeable and true,
 Of all the Life and Power,
Dispensing light in silence through
 Every successive hour,

Lord, brighten our declining day,
 That it may never wane;
Till death, when all things round decay,
 Brings back the morn again.

This grace on Thy redeem'd confer,
 Father, Co-equal Son,
And Holy Ghost, the Comforter,
 Eternal Three in one.

The Peace of God (1)

'The peace of God,' says the Apostle, 'which passeth all understanding, shall keep your hearts and minds through Christ Jesus.' There are many things in the Gospel to alarm us, many to agitate us, many to transport us, but the end and issue of all these is *peace*. 'Glory to God in the highest, and on earth peace.' It may be asked indeed whether warfare, perplexity, and uncertainty be not the condition of the Christian here below; whether St Paul himself does not say that he has 'the care', or the anxiety, 'of all the churches', and whether he does not plainly evince and avow in his Epistles to the Galatians and Corinthians much distress of mind? 'Without were fightings, within fears.' I grant it; he certainly shows at times much agitation of mind; but consider this. Did you ever look at an expanse of water and observe the ripples on the surface? Do you think that disturbance penetrates below it? Nay; you have seen or heard of fearful tempests on the sea; scenes of horror and distress, which are in no respect a fit type of an Apostle's tears or sighings about his flock. Yet even these violent commotions do not reach into the depths. The foundations of the ocean, the vast realms of water which girdle the earth, are as tranquil and as silent in the storm as in a calm. So is it with the souls of holy men.

The Peace of God (2)

The Christian has a deep, silent, hidden peace which the world sees not, like some well in a retired and shady place, difficult of access. He is the greater part of his time by himself, and when he is in solitude, that is his real state. What he is when left to himself and to his God, that is his true life. He can bear himself; he can (as it were) joy in himself, for it is the grace of God within him, it is the presence of the Eternal Comforter, in which he joys. He can bear, he finds it pleasant, to be with himself at all times, 'never less alone than when alone'. He can lay his head on his pillow at night, and own in God's sight, with overflowing heart, that he wants nothing, that he 'is full and abounds', that God has been all things to him, and that nothing is not his which God could give him. More thankfulness, more holiness, more of heaven he needs indeed, but the thought that he can have more is not a thought of trouble, but of joy. It does not interfere with his peace to know that he may grow nearer God. Such is the Christian's peace, when, with a single heart and the Cross in his eye, he addresses and commends himself to Him with whom the night is as clear as the day. St Paul says that 'the peace of God shall *keep* our hearts and minds'. By 'keep' is meant 'guard', or 'garrison', our hearts; so as to keep out enemies. And he says, our 'hearts and minds' in contrast to what the world sees of us. Many hard things may be said of the Christian, and done against him, but he has a secret preservative or charm, and minds them not.

Thy Peace Impart

O God, who canst not change nor fail,
  Guiding the hours, as they roll by,
Bright'ning with beams the morning pale,
  And burning in the mid-day sky,

Quench Thou the fires of hate and strife,
  The wasting fever of the heart;
From perils guard our feeble life,
  And to our souls Thy peace impart.

Grant this, O Father, Only Son,
  And Holy Spirit, God of grace,
To whom all glory, Three in One,
  Be given in every time and place.

Peace at the Last
THE HOPE OF HEAVEN

Everything our Hearts can Wish

What have we to do with the gifts and honours of this attractive but deceitful world, who, having been already baptized into the world to come, are no longer citizens of this? Why should we be anxious for a long life, or wealth, or credit, or comfort, who know that the next world will be everything which our hearts can wish, and that not in appearance only, but truly and everlastingly? Why should we rest in this world, when it is the token and promise of another? Why should we be content with its surface, instead of appropriating what is stored beneath it? To those who live by faith, everything they see speaks of that future world; the very glories of nature, the sun, moon, and stars, and the richness and the beauty of the earth, are as types and figures witnessing and teaching the invisible things of God. All that we see is destined one day to burst forth into a heavenly bloom, and to be transfigured into immortal glory. Heaven at present is out of sight, but in due time, as snow melts and discovers what it lay upon, so will this visible creation fade away before those greater splendours which are behind it, and on which at present it depends.

Beyond the Veil

Oh that there were such an heart in us, to put aside this visible world, to desire to look at it as a mere screen between us and God, and to think of Him who has entered in beyond the veil, and who is watching us, trying us, yes, and blessing, and influencing, and encouraging us towards good, day by day! Yet, alas, how do we suffer the mere varying circumstances of every day to sway us! How difficult it is to remain firm and in one mind under the seductions or terrors of the world! We feel variously according to the place, time, and people we are with. We are serious on Sunday, and we sin deliberately on Monday. We rise in the morning with remorse at our offences and resolutions of amendment, yet before night we have transgressed again. The mere change of society puts us into a new frame of mind; nor do we sufficiently understand this great weakness of ours, or seek for strength where alone it can be found, in the Unchangeable God. What will be our thoughts in that day, when at length this outward world drops away altogether, and we find ourselves where we ever have been, in His presence, with Christ standing at His right hand!

The Two Worlds

Unveil, O Lord, and on us shine
  In glory and in grace;
This gaudy world grows pale before
  The beauty of Thy face.

Till Thou art seen, it seems to be
  A sort of fairy ground,
Where suns unsetting light the sky,
  And flowers and fruits abound.

But when Thy keener, purer beam
  Is pour'd upon our sight,
It loses all its power to charm,
  And what was day is night.

Its noblest toils are then the scourge
  Which made Thy blood to flow;
Its joys are but the treacherous thorns
  Which circled round Thy brow.

And thus, when we renounce for Thee
  Its restless aims and fears,
The tender memories of the past,
  The hopes of coming years,

Poor is our sacrifice, whose eyes
  Are lighted from above;
We offer what we cannot keep,
  What we have ceased to love.

———

Yearning for God

The planting of Christ's Cross in the heart is sharp and trying; but the stately tree rears itself aloft, and has fair branches and rich fruit, and is good to look upon. And if all this be true even of sad or of ordinary times, much more does it hold good of seasons of religious obedience and comfort.

Such are the feelings with which men often look back on their childhood, when any accident brings it vividly before them. Some relic or token of that early time, some spot, or some book, or a word, or a scent, or a sound, brings them back in memory to the first years of their discipleship, and they then see, what they could not know at the time, that God's presence went up with them and gave them rest. Nay, even now perhaps they are unable to discern fully what it was which made that time so bright and glorious. They are full of tender, affectionate thoughts towards those first years, but they do not know why. They think it is those very years which they yearn after, whereas it is the presence of God which, as they see now, was then over them, which attracts them. They think that they regret the past, when they are but longing after the future. It is not that they would be children again, but that they would be Angels and would see God; they would be immortal beings, crowned with amaranth, robed in white, and with palms in their hands, before His throne.

———

The Greater Good

Almighty God does not bring back the past, His dispensations move forward in an equable uniform way, like circles expanding about one centre – the greater good to come being, not indeed the same as the past good, but nevertheless resembling it, as a substance resembles its type. In the past we see the future as if in miniature and outline. Indeed how can it be otherwise? seeing that all goods are but types and shadows of God Himself the Giver, and are like each other because they are like Him.

Heaven Grows out of Earth

Praise to the Holiest in the height,
  And in the depth be praise:
In all His words most wonderful;
  Most sure in all His ways! . . .

O man! albeit the quickening ray,
  Lit from his second birth,
Makes him at length what once he was,
  And heaven grows out of earth;

Yet still between that earth and heaven –
  His journey and his goal –
A double agony awaits
  His body and his soul.

A double debt he has to pay –
  The forfeit of his sins:
The chill of death is past, and now
  The penance-fire begins.

Glory to Him, who evermore
  By truth and justice reigns;
Who tears the soul from out its case,
  And burns away its stains!

As Little Children

Childhood is a type of the perfect Christian state; our Saviour so made it when He said that we must become as little children to enter His kingdom. Yet it, too, is a thing past and over. We are not, we cannot be children; grown men have faculties, passions, aims, principles, views, duties, which children have not; still, however, we must become *as* little children; in them we are bound to see Christian perfection, and to labour for it with them in our eye. Indeed there is a very much closer connection between the state of Adam in Paradise and our state in childhood than may at first be thought; so that in surveying Eden, we are in a way looking back on our own childhood; and in aiming to be children again we are aiming to be as Adam on his creation . . . Adam's state in Eden seems to have been like the state of children now – in being simple, inartificial, inexperienced in evil, unreasoning, uncalculating, ignorant of the future, or (as men now speak) un-intellectual . . .

In [both] these states the 'knowledge of good and evil' is away, whatever be the meaning of that phrase, and that instead of it the Lord is our Light, 'and in His light shall we see light'. . . Far different is our state since the fall: at present our moral rectitude, such as it is, is acquired by trial, by discipline: but what does this really mean? by sinning, by suffering, by correcting ourselves, by improving. We advance to the truth by experience of error; we succeed through failures. We know not how to do right except by having done wrong. We call virtue a mean, that is, as considering it to lie between things that are wrong. We know what is right, not positively, but negatively: we do not see the truth at once and make towards it, but we fall upon and try error, and find it is *not* the truth. We grope about by touch, not by sight, and so by a miserable experience exhaust the possible modes of acting till nought is left, but truth, remaining. Such is the process by which we succeed; we walk to heaven backward . . .

A Pledge of Immortality

What we were when children is a blessed *intimation*, given for our comfort, of what God will make us if we surrender our hearts to the guidance of His Holy Spirit: a prophecy of good to come; a foretaste of what will be fulfilled in heaven. And thus it is that a child is a pledge of immortality; for he bears upon him in figure those high and eternal excellences in which the joy of heaven consists, and which would not be thus shadowed forth by the All-gracious Creator, were they not one day to be realized.

An Intimation of Eternity

All the points in which men differ, health and strength, high or low estate, happiness or misery, vanish before this common lot, mortality.

And this sense of the nothingness of life, impressed on us by the very fact that it comes to an end, is much deepened, when we contrast it with the capabilities of us who live it. Had Jacob lived Methuselah's age, he would have called it short. This is what we all feel, though at first sight it seems a contradiction, that even though the days as they go be slow, and be laden with many events, or with sorrows or dreariness, lengthening them out and making them tedious, yet the year passes quick though the hours tarry, and time bygone is as a dream, though we thought it would never go while it was going. And the reason seems to be this; that, when we contemplate human life in itself, in however small a portion of it, we see implied in it the presence of a soul, the energy of a spiritual existence, of an accountable being; consciousness tells us this concerning it every moment. But when we look back on it in memory, we view it but externally, as a mere lapse of time, as a mere earthly history. And the longest duration of this external world is as dust, and weighs nothing against one moment's life of the world within. Thus we are ever expecting great things from life, from our internal consciousness every moment of our having souls; and we are ever being disappointed, on considering what we have gained from time past, or can hope from time to come. . . .

Our earthly life, then, gives promise of what it does not accomplish. It promises immortality, yet it is mortal; it contains life in death and eternity in time; and it attracts us by beginnings which faith alone brings to an end. I mean, when we take into account the powers with which our souls are gifted as Christians, the very consciousness of these fills us with a certainty that they must last beyond this life; that is, in the case of good and holy men, whose present state, I say, is to them who know them well, an earnest of immortality. The greatness of their gifts, contrasted with their scanty time for exercising them, forces the mind forward to the thought of another life, as almost the necessary counterpart and consequence of this life, and certainly implied in this life, provided there be a righteous Governor of the world who does not make man for nought.

What a Day

What a day will that be when I am thoroughly cleansed from all impurity and sin, and am fit to draw near to my Incarnate God in His palace of light above! What a morning, when having done with all penal suffering, I see Thee for the first time with these very eyes of mine, I see thy countenance, gaze upon Thy eyes and gracious lips without quailing, and then kneel down with joy to kiss Thy feet, and am welcomed into Thy arms. O my only true lover, the only Lover of my soul, Thee will I love now, that I may love Thee then. What a day, a long day without ending, the day of eternity, when I shall be so unlike what I am *now*, when I feel in myself a body of death, and am perplexed, and distracted with ten thousand thoughts, any one of which would keep me from heaven. O my Lord, what a day when I shall have done once for all with all sins, venial as well as mortal, and shall stand perfect and acceptable in Thy sight, able to bear Thy presence, nothing shrinking from Thy eye, not shrinking from the pure scrutiny of Angels and Archangels, when I stand in the midst and they around me.

———

God's Hidden Kingdom

The earth that we see does not satisfy us; it is but a beginning; it is but a promise of something beyond it; even when it is gayest, with all its blossoms on, and shows most touchingly what lies hid in it, yet it is not enough. We know much more lies hid in it than we see. A world of Saints and Angels, a glorious world, the palace of God, the mountain of the Lord of Hosts, the heavenly Jerusalem, the throne of God and Christ, all these wonders, everlasting, all-precious, mysterious, and incomprehensible, lie hid in what we see. What we see is the outward shell of an eternal kingdom; and on that kingdom we fix the eyes of our faith. Shine forth, O Lord, as when on Thy Nativity Thine Angels visited the shepherds; let Thy glory blossom forth as bloom and foliage on the trees; change with Thy mighty power this visible world into that diviner world, which as yet we see not; destroy what we see, that it may pass and be transformed into what we believe. Bright as is the sun, and the sky, and the clouds; green as are the leaves and the fields; sweet as is the singing of the birds; we know that they are not all, and we will not take up with a part for the whole. They proceed from a centre of love and goodness, which is God himself; but they are not His fullness; they speak of heaven, but they are not heaven; they are but as stray beams and dim reflections of His Image; they are but crumbs from the table.

———

The Holy Jerusalem

O happy they who, in a sorrowful time, avail themselves of this bond of communion with the Saints of old and with the Universal Church! O wise and dutiful who, when the world has robbed them of so much, set the more account upon what remains! We have not lost all, while we have the dwelling-places of our forefathers; while we can repair those which are broken down, and build upon the old foundations and propagate them upon new sites! Happy they who, when they enter within their holy limits, enter in heart into the court of heaven! And most unhappy who, while they have eyes to admire, admire them only for their beauty's sake and the skill they exhibit; who regard them as works of art, not fruits of grace; bow down before their material forms, instead of worshipping 'in spirit and in truth'; count their stones, and measure their spaces, but discern in them no tokens of the invisible, no canons of truth, no lessons of wisdom, to guide them forward in the way heavenward!

In heaven is the substance, of which here below we are vouchsafed the image; and thither, if we be worthy, we shall at length attain. There is the holy Jerusalem, whose light is like unto a stone most precious, even like a jasper stone, clear as crystal; and whose wall is great and high, with twelve gates, and an Angel at each – whose glory is the Lord God Almighty, and the Lamb is the light thereof.

The Temple of God

We are apt to deceive ourselves, and to consider heaven a place like this earth; I mean, a place where everyone may choose and take his *own* pleasure. We see that in this world, active men have their own enjoyments, and domestic men have theirs; men of literature, of science, of political talent, have their respective pursuits and pleasures. Hence we are led to act as if it will be the same in another world. The only difference we put between this world and the next, is that *here* (as we know well) men are *not always sure*, but *there*, we suppose they *will be always sure*, of obtaining what they seek after. And accordingly we conclude, that *any man*, whatever his habits, tastes, or manner of life, if *once admitted* into heaven, would be happy there. Not that we altogether deny that some preparation is necessary for the next world; but we do not estimate its real extent and importance. We think we can reconcile ourselves to God when we will; as if nothing were required in the case of men in general, but some temporary attention, more than ordinary, to our religious duties – some strictness, during our last sickness, in the services of the Church, as men of business arrange their letters and papers on taking a journey or balancing an account. But an opinion like this, though commonly acted on, is refuted as soon as put into words. For heaven, it is plain from Scripture, is not a place where many different and discordant pursuits can be carried on at once, as is the case in this world. Here every man can do his *own* pleasure, but there he must do *God's* pleasure. It would be presumption to attempt to determine the employments of that eternal life which good men are to pass in God's presence, or to deny that that state which eye hath not seen, nor ear heard, nor mind conceived, may comprise an infinite variety of pursuits and occupations. Still so far we are distinctly told, that that future life will be spent in God's *presence*, in a sense which does not apply to our present life; so that it may be best described as an endless and uninterrupted worship of the Eternal Father, Son, and Spirit. 'They serve Him day and night in His temple, and He that sitteth on the throne shall dwell among them . . .'

———

God is All

God alone is in heaven; God is all in all. Eternal Lord, I acknowledge this truth, and I adore Thee in this sovereign and most glorious mystery. There is One God, and He fills Heaven; and all blessed creatures, though they ever remain in their individuality, are, as the very means of their blessedness, absorbed, and (as it were) drowned in the fullness of Him who is *super omnes, et per omnia, et in omnibus.* If ever, through Thy grace, I attain to see Thee in heaven, I shall see nothing else but Thee, because I shall see all whom I see in Thee, and seeing them I shall see Thee. As I cannot see things here below without light, and to see them is to see the rays which come from them, so in that Eternal City *claritas Dei illuminavit eam, et lucerna ejus est Agnus* – the glory of God hath enlightened it, and the Lamb is the lamp thereof.

The Language of Heaven

I say, then, it is plain to common sense that the man who has not accustomed himself to the language of heaven will be no fit inhabitant of it when, in the Last Day, it is perceptibly revealed. The case is like that of a language or style of speaking of this world; we know well a foreigner from a native. Again, we know those who have been used to kings' courts or educated society from others. By their voice, accent, and language, and not only so, by their gestures and gait, by their usages, by their mode of conducting themselves and their principles of conduct, we know well what a vast difference there is between those who have lived in good society and those who have not. What indeed is called 'good society' is often very worthless society. I am not speaking of it to praise it; I only mean, that, as the manners which men call refined or courtly are gained only by intercourse with courts and polished circles, and as the influence of the words there used (that is, of the ideas which those words, striking again and again on the ear, convey to the mind), extends in a most subtle way over all that men do, over the turn of their sentences, and the tone of their questions and replies, and their general bearing, and the spontaneous flow of their thoughts, and their mode of viewing things, and the general maxims or heads to which they refer them, and the motives which determine them, and their likings and dislikings, hopes and fears, and their relative estimate of persons, and the intensity of their perceptions towards particular objects; so a habit of prayer, the practice of turning to God and the unseen world, in every season, in every place, in every emergency, prayer, I say, has what may be called a *natural* effect, in spiritualizing and elevating the soul. A man is no longer what he was before; gradually, imperceptibly to himself, he has imbibed a new set of ideas, and becomes imbued with fresh principles. He is as one coming from kings' courts, with a grace, a delicacy, a dignity, a propriety, a justness of thought and taste, a clearness and firmness of principle, all his own. Such is the power of God's secret grace acting through those ordinances which He has enjoined us. As speech is the organ of human society, and the means of human civilization, so is prayer the instrument of divine fellowship and divine training.

None but the Holy

If then a man without religion (supposing it possible) were admitted into heaven, doubtless he would sustain a great disappointment. Before, indeed, he fancied that he could be happy there; but when he arrived there, he would find no discourse but that which he had shunned on earth, no pursuits but those he had disliked or despised, nothing which bound him to aught *else* in the universe, and made him feel at home, nothing which he could enter into and rest upon. He would perceive himself to be an isolated being, cut away by Supreme Power from those objects which were still entwined around his heart. Nay, he would be in the presence of that Supreme Power, whom he never on earth could bring himself steadily to think upon, and whom now he regarded only as the destroyer of all that was precious and dear to him. Ah! he could not *bear* the face of the Living God; the Holy God would be no object of joy to him. 'Let us alone! What have we to do with thee?' is the sole thought and desire of unclean souls, even while they acknowledge His majesty. None but the holy can look upon the Holy One; without holiness no man can endure to see the Lord.

When, then, we think to take part in the joys of heaven without holiness, we are as inconsiderate as if we supposed we could take an interest in the worship of Christians here below without possessing it in our measure. A careless, a sensual, an unbelieving mind, a mind destitute of the love and fear of God, with narrow views and earthly aims, a low standard of duty, and a benighted conscience, a mind contented with itself, and unresigned to God's will, would feel as little pleasure, at the last day, at the words, 'Enter into the joy of thy Lord', as it does now at the words, 'Let us pray'. Nay, much less, because, while we are in a church, we may turn our thoughts to other subjects, and contrive to forget that God is looking on us; but that will not be possible in heaven.

For the Dead

Help, Lord, the souls which Thou hast made,
  The souls to Thee so dear,
In prison for the debt unpaid
  Of sins committed here.

Those holy souls, they suffer on,
  Resign'd in heart and will,
Until Thy high behest is done,
  And justice has its fill.
For daily falls, for pardon'd crime,
  They joy to undergo
The shadow of Thy cross sublime,
  The remnant of Thy woe.

Help, Lord, the souls which Thou hast made,
  The souls to Thee so dear,
In prison for the debt unpaid
  Of sins committed here.

Oh, by their patience of delay,
  Their hope amid their pain,
Their sacred zeal to burn away
  Disfigurement and stain;
Oh, by their fire of love, not less
  In keenness than the flame,
Oh, by their very helplessness,
  Oh, by Thy own great Name,

Good Jesu, help! sweet Jesu, aid
  The souls to Thee most dear,
In prison for the debt unpaid
  Of sins committed here.

True Faithfulness

The word *faithfulness* means loyalty to a superior, or exactness in fulfilling an engagement. In the latter sense it is applied even to Almighty God Himself, who, in His great love for us, has vouchsafed to limit His own power in action by His word of promise and His covenant with His creatures. He has given His word that, if we will take Him for our portion and put ourselves into His hands, He will guide us through all trials and temptations, and bring us safe to heaven. And to encourage and inspirit us, He reminds us, in various passages of Scripture, that He is the *faithful* God, the *faithful* Creator.

And so, His true saints and servants have the special title of 'Faithful', as being true to Him as He is to them; as being simply obedient to His will, zealous for His honour, observant of the sacred interests which He has committed to their keeping. Thus Abraham is called the Faithful; Moses is declared to be faithful in all his house; David, on this account, is called the 'man after God's own heart'; St Paul returns thanks that 'God accounted him faithful'; and, at the last day, God will say to all those who have well employed their talents, 'Well done, good and faithful servant.'

Joy Unspeakable

Let us steadily contemplate the mystery, and say whether any consequence is too great to follow from so marvellous a dispensation; any mystery so great, any grace so overpowering, as that which is already manifested in the incarnation and death of the Eternal Son. Were we told that the effect of it would be to make us as Seraphim, that we were to ascend as high as He descended low – would that startle us after the Angel's news to the shepherds? And this indeed is the effect of it, so far as such words may be spoken without impiety. Men we remain, but not mere men, but gifted with a measure of all those perfections which Christ has in fullness, partaking each in his own degree of His Divine Nature so fully, that the only reason (so to speak) why His saints are not really like Him, is that it is impossible – that He is the Creator, and they His creatures; yet still so, that they are all but Divine, all that they can be made without violating the incommunicable majesty of the Most High. Surely in proportion to His glory is His power of glorifying; so that to say that through Him we shall be made *all but* gods – though it is to say, that we are infinitely below the adorable Creator – still is to say, and truly, that we shall be higher than every other being in the world; higher than Angels or Archangels, Cherubim or Seraphim – that is, not here, or in ourselves, but in heaven and in Christ – Christ, already the first-fruits of our race, God and man, having ascended high above all creatures, and we through His grace tending to the same high blessedness, having the earnest of His glory given here, and (if we be found faithful) the fullness of it hereafter.

If all these things be so, surely the lesson of joy which the Incarnation gives us is as impressive as the lesson of humility. St Paul gives us the one lesson in his Epistle to the Philippians: 'Let this mind be in you, which was also in Christ Jesus: who, being in the form of God, thought it not robbery to be equal with God: but made Himself of no reputation, and took upon Him the form of a servant, and was made in the likeness of men': and St Peter gives us the lesson of joyfulness: 'Whom having not seen, ye love; in whom, though now ye see Him not, yet believing, ye rejoice with joy unspeakable, and full of glory: receiving the end of your faith, even the salvation of your souls.'

Satisfied in Spirit

When with their fleshly eyes and ears the Apostles saw Him no more, when He had ascended whither flesh and blood cannot enter, and the barrier of the flesh was interposed between Him and them, how should they any longer see and hear Him? 'Lord, whither goest Thou?' they said; and He answered to Peter, 'Whither I go thou canst not follow Me now, but thou shalt follow Me afterwards.' They were to follow Him through the veil, and to break the barrier of the flesh after His pattern. They must, as far as they could, weaken and attenuate what stood between them and Him; they must anticipate that world where flesh and blood are not; they must discern truths which flesh and blood could not reveal; they must live a life, not of sense, but of spirit; they must practise those mortifications which former religions had enjoined, which the Pharisees and John's disciples observed, with better fruit, for a higher end, in a more heavenly way, in order to see Him who is invisible. By fasting, Moses saw God's glory; by fasting, Elijah heard the 'still small voice'; by fasting, Christ's disciples were to express their mourning over the Crucified and Dead, over the Bridegroom taken away: but that mourning would bring Him back, that mourning would be turned to joy; in that mourning they would see Him, they would hear of Him, again; they would see Him, as they mourned and wept. And while they mourned, so long would they see Him and rejoice – for 'blessed are they that mourn, for they shall be comforted'; they are 'sorrowful, yet always rejoicing'; hungering and thirsting after and unto righteousness – fasting in body, that their soul may hunger and thirst after its true good; fasting in body, that they may be satisfied in spirit; in a 'barren and dry land, where no water is', that they may look for Him in holiness, and behold His power and glory.

God Alone

My Lord is gone up into heaven. I adore Thee, Son of Mary, Jesu Emmanuel, my God and my Saviour. I am allowed to adore Thee, my Saviour and my own Brother, for Thou art God. I follow Thee in my thoughts, O Thou First-fruits of our race, as I hope one day by Thy grace to follow Thee in my person. To go to heaven is to go to God. God is there and God alone: for perfect bliss is there and nothing else, and none can be blessed who is not bathed and hidden and absorbed in the glory of the Divine Nature. All holy creatures are but the vestment of the Highest, which He has put on for ever, and which is bright with His uncreated light. There are many things on earth, and each is its own centre, but one Name alone is named above. It is God alone. This is that true supernatural life; and if I would live a supernatural life on earth, and attain to the supernatural eternal life which is in heaven, I have one thing to do, viz., to live on the thought of God here. Teach me this, O God; give me Thy supernatural grace to practise it; to have my reason, affections, intentions, aims, all penetrated and possessed by the love of Thee, plunged and drowned in the one Vision of Thee.

Not of this World

We should remember that this life is scarcely more than an accident of our being – that it is no part of ourselves, who are immortal; that we are immortal spirits, independent of time and space, and that this life is but a sort of outward stage, on which we act for a time, and which is only sufficient and only intended to answer the purpose of trying whether we will serve God or no. We should consider ourselves to be in this world in no fuller sense than players in any game are in the game; and life to be a sort of dream, as detached and as different from our real eternal existence, as a dream differs from waking; a serious dream, indeed, as affording a means of judging us, yet in itself a kind of shadow without substance, a scene set before us, in which we seem to be, and in which it is our duty to act just as if all we saw had a truth and reality, because all that meets us influences us and our destiny. The regenerate soul is taken into communion with Saints and Angels, and its 'life is hid with Christ in God'; it has a place in God's court, and is not of this world – looking into this world as a spectator might look at some show or pageant except when called from time to time to take a part. And while it obeys the instinct of the senses, it does so for God's sake, and it submits itself to things of time so far as to be brought to perfection by them, that, when the veil is withdrawn and it sees itself to be, where it ever has been, in God's kingdom, it may be found worthy to enjoy it.

The Last Time

Ever since Christianity came into the world, it has been, in one sense, going out of it. It is so uncongenial to the human mind, it is so spiritual, and man is so earthly, it is apparently so defenceless, and has so many strong enemies, so many false friends, that every age, as it comes, may be called 'the last time'. It has made great conquests, and done great works; but still it has done all, as the Apostle says of himself, 'in weakness, and in fear, and in much trembling'. *How* it is that it is always failing, yet always continuing, God only knows who wills it – but so it is; and it is no paradox to say, on the one hand, that it has lasted eighteen hundred years, that it may last many years more, and yet that it draws to an end, nay, is likely to end any day. And God would have us give our minds and hearts to the latter side of the alternative, to open them to impressions *from* this side, viz. that the end is coming – it being a wholesome thing to live as if *that* will come in our day, which may come any day.

———

In Prospect of Death

I write in the direct view of death as in prospect. No one in the house, I suppose, suspects anything of the kind. Nor anyone anywhere, unless it be the medical men.

I write at once – because, on my own feelings of mind and body, it is as if nothing at all were the matter with me, just now; but because I do not know how long this perfect possession of my sensible and available health and strength may last.

I die in the faith of the One Holy Catholic Apostolic Church. I trust I shall die prepared and protected by her Sacraments, which our Lord Jesus Christ has committed to her, and in that communion of Saints which He inaugurated when He ascended on high, and which will have no end. I hope to die in that Church which our Lord founded on Peter, and which will continue till His second coming.

MONTH SIX : DAY TWENTY-FIVE

———

Prayer for a Happy Death

Oh, my Lord and Saviour, support me in that hour in the strong arms of Thy Sacraments, and by the fresh fragrance of Thy consolations. Let the absolving words be said over me, and the holy oil sign and seal me, and Thy own Body be my food, and Thy Blood my sprinkling; and let my sweet Mother, Mary, breathe on me, and my Angel whisper peace to me, and my glorious Saints . . . smile upon me; that in them all, and through them all, I may receive the gift of perseverance, and die, as I desire to live, in Thy faith, in Thy Church, in Thy service, and in Thy love. Amen.

A Dream

She slept sound; she dreamed . . . She thought she saw before her a well-known face, only glorified. She, who had been a slave, now was arrayed more brilliantly than an oriental queen; and she looked at Callista with a smile so sweet, that Callista felt she could but dance to it.

And as she looked more earnestly, doubting whether she should begin or not, the face changed, and now was more marvellous still. It had an innocence in its look, and also a tenderness, which bespoke both Maid and Mother, and so transported Callista, that she must needs advance towards her, out of love and reverence. And the lady seemed to make signs of encouragement: so she began a solemn measure, unlike all dances of earth, with hands and feet, serenely moving on towards what she heard some of them call a great action and a glorious consummation, though she did not know what they meant. At length she was fain to sing as well as dance; and her words were, 'In the name of the Father, and of the Son and of the Holy Ghost'; on which another said, 'A good beginning of the sacrifice'. And when she had come close to this gracious figure, there was a fresh change. The face, the features were the same; but the light of Divinity now seemed to beam through them, and the hair parted, and hung down long on each side of the forehead; and there was a crown of another fashion than the Lady's round about it, made of what looked like thorns. And the palms of the hands were spread out as if towards her, and there were marks of wounds in them. And the vestment had fallen, and there was a deep opening in the side. And as she stood entranced before Him, and motionless, she felt a consciousness that her own palms were pierced like His, and her feet also. And she looked round, and saw the likeness of His face and of His wounds upon all that company. And now they were suddenly moving on, and bearing something or some one, heavenwards; and they too began to sing, and their words seemed to be, 'Rejoice with Me, for I have found My sheep', ever repeated. They went up through an avenue or long grotto, with torches of diamonds, and amethysts, and sapphires, which lit up its spars and made them sparkle. And she tried to look, but could not discover what they were carrying, till she heard a very piercing cry, which awoke her.

———

Regeneration

I went to sleep; and now I am refresh'd,
A strange refreshment: for I feel in me
An inexpressive lightness, and a sense
Of freedom, as I were at length myself,
And ne'er had been before. How still it is!
I hear no more the busy beat of time,
No, nor my fluttering breath, nor struggling pulse;
Nor does one moment differ from the next.
I had a dream; yes: some one softly said
'He's gone'; and then a sigh went round the room.
And then I surely heard a priestly voice
Cry '*Subvenite*'; and they knelt in prayer.
I seem to hear him still; but thin and low,
And fainter and more faint the accents come,
As at an ever-widening interval.
Ah! whence is this? What is this severance?
This silence pours a solitariness
Into the very essence of my soul;
And the deep rest, so soothing and so sweet,
Hath something too of sternness and of pain.
For it drives back my thoughts upon their spring
By a strange introversion, and perforce
I now begin to feed upon myself,
Because I have nought else to feed upon.

———

Go, Christian Soul!

Proficiscere, anima Christiana, de hoc mundo!
Go forth upon thy journey, Christian soul!
Go from this world! Go, in the Name of God
The Omnipotent Father, who created thee!
Go, in the Name of Jesus Christ, our Lord,
Son of the living God, who bled for thee!
Go, in the Name of the Holy Spirit, who
Hath been pour'd out on thee! Go, in the name
Of Angels and Archangels; in the name
Of Thrones and Dominations; in the name
Of Princedoms and of Powers; and in the name
Of Cherubim and Seraphim, go forth!
Go, in the name of Patriarchs and Prophets;
And of Apostles and Evangelists,
Of Martyrs and Confessors; in the name
Of holy Monks and Hermits; in the name
Of Holy Virgins; and all Saints of God,
Both men and women, go! Go on thy course;
And may thy place today be found in peace,
And may thy dwelling be the Holy Mount
Of Sion – through the Same, through Christ, our Lord.

The Golden Prison

Weep not for me, when I am gone,
Nor spend thy faithful breath
In grieving o'er the spot or hour
Of all-enshrouding death;

Nor waste in idle praise thy love
On deeds of head or hand,
Which live within the living Book,
Or else are writ in sand;

But let it be thy best of prayers,
That I may find the grace
To reach the holy house of toll
The frontier penance-place –

To reach that golden palace bright,
Where souls elect abide,
Waiting their certain call to Heaven,
With Angels at their side;

Where hate, nor pride, nor fear torments
The transitory guest,
But in the willing agony
He plunges, and is blest.

And as the fainting patriarch gain'd
His needful halt mid-way,
And then refresh'd pursued his path,
Where up the mount it lay,

So pray, that, rescued from the storm
Of heaven's eternal ire,
I may lie down, then rise again
Safe, and yet saved by fire.

———

Peace at the Last

O Lord, support us all the day long of this troublous life, until the shades lengthen, and the evening comes, and the busy world is hushed, the fever of life is over, and our work is done. Then, Lord, in thy mercy grant us safe lodging, a holy rest, and peace at the last; through Jesus Christ our Lord. Amen.

Sources

Unless otherwise stated, quotations have been taken from works included by Newman in the uniform edition published by Longmans, Green and Co. between 1868 and 1881.

MONTH ONE

1 Letter to Mrs William Froude, 23.2.1853, *Letters and Diaries of John Henry Newman* (31 vols, eds. C. S. Dessain, I. Ker, T. Gornall, Oxford University Press 1972–84), xv.
2 *Apologia pro Vita Sua* (1873), pp. 241–3.
3 *The Idea of a University defined and illustrated* (1873).
4 *Parochial and Plain Sermons* (1868), i, pp. 42–3.
5 *Apologia*, p. 198.
6 *The Idea of a University*, pp. 25–7.
7 *Parochial and Plain Sermons*, iv, p. 293.
8 *The Idea of a University*, pp. 63–5.
9 *The Idea of a University*.
10 *Discussions and Arguments on Various Subjects* (1872), pp. 211–12.
11 *Fifteen Sermons preached before the University of Oxford (University Sermons)* (1872).
12 *The Idea of a University*.
13 *Essays Critical and Historical* (1871), i, pp. 31–2, 33.
14 Letter to W S Lilly, 7.12.1882, *Letters and Diaries*, xxx.
15 Letter to H A Woodgate, 23.2.1872, *Letters and Diaries*, xxvi.
16 *An Essay in aid of a Grammar of Assent* (1870), pp. 116–18.
17 *Grammar of Assent*, pp. 130–1.
18 *Grammar of Assent*, pp. 219–20.
19 *Parochial and Plain Sermons*.
20 *Parochial and Plain Sermons*, iv, p. 257.
21 *Lectures on the Doctrine of Justification* (1874).
22 *Parochial and Plain Sermons*, iii, p. 161.
23 *Parochial and Plain Sermons*, v.
24 *Meditations and Devotions of the late Cardinal Newman*, Longmans, Green and Co., 1893.
25 *Parochial and Plain Sermons*, ii, p. 67.
26 Letter to Mrs J Mozley, 15.3.1845, *Letters and Correspondence of John Henry Newman*, ed. Anne Mozley, Longmans, Green and Co., 1891, p. 459.
27 *Parochial and Plain Sermons*, v, pp. 83–4.
28 *The Idea of a University*, pp. 518–19.
29 *Grammar of Assent*, pp. 132–3.
30 'The Dream of Gerontius', *Verses on Various Occasions* (1874), p. 230.

MONTH TWO

1 *Parochial and Plain Sermons*, iv, pp. 227–8.
2 *Meditations and Devotions*, pp. 497–8.
3 *Parochial and Plain Sermons*, iv, p. 31.
4 *Meditations and Devotions*, p. 594.
5 *Parochial and Plain Sermons*, v.
6 *Meditations and Devotions*, pp. 600–1.
7 *Parochial and Plain Sermons*, vii, p. 205–11.
8 *Meditations and Devotions*, p. 592.
9 *Parochial and Plain Sermons*, vi, pp. 42–3.
10 *Meditations and Devotions*, pp. 571–12.
11 *Parochial and Plain Sermons*, v, pp. 25–6.
12 *Meditations and Devotions*.
13 *Sermons preached on Various Occasions* (1870), pp. 34–7.
14 *Meditations and Devotions*, pp. 495–6.
15 *Parochial and Plain Sermons*, iv, p. 322.
16 *Verses on Various Occasions*, p. 131.
17 *Loss and Gain: the Story of a Convert* (1874).
18 *Meditations and Devotions*.
19 *Parochial and Plain Sermons*, iv, p. 339.
20 *Meditations and Devotions*.
21 *Verses on Various Occasions*, p. 54.
22 *Meditations and Devotions*.
23 *Meditations and Devotions*, pp. 78–9.
24 *Meditations and Devotions*, pp. 494–5.
25 Letter to Miss Hope-Scott, 29.10.1872, *Letters and Diaries*, xxvi.
26 *Meditations and Devotions*.
27 *Parochial and Plain Sermons*, viii.
28 *Meditations and Devotions*.
29 'The Dream of Gerontius', *Verses on Various Occasions*, p. 223.
30 *Meditations and Devotions*, pp. 294–5.

MONTH THREE

1 *Parochial and Plain Sermons*, iii, pp. 119–20.
2 *Parochial and Plain Sermons*, ii, p. 30.
3 *Parochial and Plain Sermons*, ii, p. 32.
4 *Parochial and Plain Sermons*, iv, p. 240.
5 *Parochial and Plain Sermons*, iv, p. 241.
6 *Parochial and Plain Sermons*, vii.
7 *Meditations and Devotions.*
8 *Essays Critical and Historical*, i, pp. 249–51.
9 *Parochial and Plain Sermons*, iv, p. 252.
10 *Meditations and Devotions*, p. 227.
11 'The Dream of Gerontius', *Verses on Various Occasions*, pp. 265–6.
12 *Parochial and Plain Sermons*, vii, pp. 89–90.
13 *Verses on Various Occasions*, pp. 188–9.
14 *Lectures on Justification.*
15 *Verses on Various Occasions*, p. 113.
16 *Letters and Diaries.*
17 *Meditations and Devotions*, pp. 245–6.
18 *Parochial and Plain Sermons*, viii, pp. 231–3.
19 *Parochial and Plain Sermons*, i, pp. 288–90.
20 *Meditations and Devotions*, pp. 330–1.
21 *Meditations and Devotions*, pp. 331–3.
22 *Lectures on Justification*, pp. 216–17, 218–19.
23 *Parochial and Plain Sermons*, ii, p. 215.
24 *Parochial and Plain Sermons*, vi, p. 22.
25 *Parochial and Plain Sermons*, vii, p. 113.
26 *University Sermons*, pp. 27–8.
27 *Lectures on Justification.*
28 *Meditations and Devotions*, p. 352.
29 *Parochial and Plain Sermons*, vii, pp. 25–6.
30 *Meditations and Devotions*, pp. 313–14.

MONTH FOUR

1 *Parochial and Plain Sermons*, vii, p. 23.
2 *Parochial and Plain Sermons*, viii, p. 24.
3 *Parochial and Plain Sermons*, v, p. 349.
4 Letter to Walter Mayers, January 1821, *Letters and Diaries*, i.
5 *Parochial and Plain Sermons*, viii, p. 130.
6 *Parochial and Plain Sermons*, viii.
7 *Grammar of Assent*.
8 *The Idea of a University*, pp. 122–3.
9 *Parochial and Plain Sermons*, i, p. 333.
10 *Parochial and Plain Sermons*, iii, p. 147.
11 *Meditations and Devotions*, pp. 52–4.
12 Letter to Mrs Elizabeth Newman, August 1835, *Letters and Correspondence*, pp. 130–1.
13 *Parochial and Plain Sermons*, vii, p. 21.
14 *Parochial and Plain Sermons*, vii, p. 32.
15 *The Idea of a University*, pp. 208–10.
16 *Parochial and Plain Sermons*, ii.
17 *Parochial and Plain Sermons*, iv, p. 325.
18 *Parochial and Plain Sermons*, vii, p. 34.
19 *Parochial and Plain Sermons*.
20 *Parochial and Plain Sermons*.
21 *Parochial and Plain Sermons*, ii, p. 347.
22 *Parochial and Plain Sermons*, ii, p. 349.
23 *Parochial and Plain Sermons*, ii, p. 346.
24 *Parochial and Plain Sermons*, iv, p. 42.
25 *Parochial and Plain Sermons*, viii, p. 168.
26 *Parochial and Plain Sermons*, viii, p. 169.
27 *Parochial and Plain Sermons*, iv.
28 Letter to Mrs J Mozley, 24.11.1844, *Letters and Correspondence*, p. 445.
29 *Apologia*, p. 169.
30 *Parochial and Plain Sermons*, iv, p. 261.

1 *Meditations and Devotions.*
2 *Parochial and Plain Sermons,* v.
3 *Meditations and Devotions,* pp. 37–9.
4 *Parochial and Plain Sermons,* v.
5 *Verses on Various Occasions,* pp. 49–50.
6 *Parochial and Plain Sermons,* v.
7 *Parochial and Plain Sermons,* v.
8 *Parochial and Plain Sermons,* v, pp. 140–2.
9 *Meditations and Devotions,* pp. 508–9.
10 *Apologia,* p. 4.
11 *Parochial and Plain Sermons,* v, p. 225.
12 *Callista, a Tale of the Third Century* (1876).
13 *Meditations and Devotions,* p. 386.
14 *Parochial and Plain Sermons.*
15 Letter to Mrs J Mozley, 15.3.1845, *Letters and Correspondence,* pp. 460–1.
16 *Parochial and Plain Sermons,* iv.
17 *Verses on Various Occasions,* p. 114.
18 *Parochial and Plain Sermons,* ii, p. 241.
19 *Parochial and Plain Sermons,* ii, p. 3.
20 *Meditations and Devotions,* pp. 381–2.
21 *Parochial and Plain Sermons,* vi, pp. 319–20, 324–5.
22 *Verses on Various Occasions,* p. 68.
23 *Parochial and Plain Sermons,* ii, p. 128.
24 *Parochial and Plain Sermons,* ii, p. 127.
25 *Parochial and Plain Sermons,* ii, p. 130.
26 *Parochial and Plain Sermons,* iv, p. 64.
27 *Verses on Various Occasions,* p. 174.
28 *Parochial and Plain Sermons,* v, p. 67.
29 *Parochial and Plain Sermons,* v, p. 70.
30 *Verses on Various Occasions,* p. 173.

MONTH SIX

1 *Parochial and Plain Sermons,* iv, p. 223.
2 *Parochial and Plain Sermons,* i, p. 25.
3 *Verses on Various Occasions,* pp. 223–4.
4 *Parochial and Plain Sermons.*
5 *Parochial and Plain Sermons,* v, p. 100.
6 'The Dream of Gerontius', *Verses on Various Occasions,* pp. 259–60.
7 *Parochial and Plain Sermons,* v, pp. 102–3, 107–9.
8 *Parochial and Plain Sermons,* ii, p. 67.
9 *Parochial and Plain Sermons,* iv, p. 216.
10 *Meditations and Devotions.*
11 *Parochial and Plain Sermons,* iv.
12 *Parochial and Plain Sermons,* i, p. 3.
13 *Meditations and Devotions.*
14 *Meditations and Devotions,* pp. 586–7.
15 *Parochial and Plain Sermons,* viii, p. 18.
16 *Parochial and Plain Sermons,* i, pp. 6–7.
17 *Verses on Various Occasions,* pp. 220–1.
18 *Meditations and Devotions.*
19 *Parochial and Plain Sermons,* viii, p. 18.
20 *Parochial and Plain Sermons,* vi, pp. 31–2.
21 *Meditations and Devotions,* pp. 535–6.
22 *Parochial and Plain Sermons,* iv.
23 *Parochial and Plain Sermons,* iv, pp. 239–40.
24 *Meditations and Devotions,* pp. 607–9.
25 *Meditations and Devotions,* p. 388.
26 *Callista.*
27 'The Dream of Gerontius', *Verses on Various Occasions,* pp. 234–5.
28 'The Dream of Gerontius', *Verses on Various Occasions,* pp. 233–4.
29 *Verses on Various Occasions,* p. 212–13.
30 This prayer is traditionally attributed to Newman and even if it was not composed by him it bears the stamp of his mind. He may have translated it from an older collect.